Good, Evil and Beyond...

Kamma in the Buddha's Teaching

by **Bhikkhu P. A. Payutto**

Translated from the Thai by Bhikkhu Puriso

Buddhadhamma Foundation
Bangkok, Thailand.

Good, Evil and Beyond . . .
Kamma in the Buddha's Teaching
© *Bhikkhu P. A. Payutto*
ISBN 974-575-262-2

First published
January, 1993

Published by
Buddhadhamma Foundation Publications
87/126 Tedsabarn-songgroh Rd.,
Chatuchak, Bangkok 10900, Thailand.
Tel: 589-9012, 580-2719
Fax: 580-5127

Cover : Design by Panya Vijinthanasarn

Printed by :   MAHACHULALONGKORNRAJVIDYALAYA
BUDDHIST UNIVERSITY PRESS
WAT MAHADHATU, BANGKOK 10200, THAILAND
Tel. 224-8214, 221-8892
FAX. 224-8214

Kamma is what we own,
Kamma do we inherit,
From kamma are we born,
and to kamma are we related.
By kamma are we supported.

All beings are the owners of their kamma
heirs of their kamma
born of their kamma
related to their kamma
supported by their kamma ...

ACKNOWLEDGEMENT

VENERABLE Puriso Bhikkhu, of Wat Pah Wana Potiyahn, Ubol Rachathani province, has been inspired to translate the chapter on *Kamma,* which makes up one chapter in the book *Buddha Dhamma,* into English, in order to transmit an understanding of the Buddhist Law of *Kamma* to peoples of other nationalities, particularly Westerners. Hopefully this will serve to encourage wiser conduct in the modern world, experiencing as it is so many problems in this direction. In addition, this book seeks to correct a number of misunderstandings of the word *kamma* that have arisen as the word becomes more widely known.

As the translator has pointed out in his own introduction, this work is not a direct translation of the original Thai version, but has been adapted to suit a Western audience. Some parts have been deleted, some trimmed down, some have been re-arranged, and there have been a number of footnotes added to explain concepts which might not be readily understood by a Western readership. Even so, the essential meaning of the original remains intact, and in fact the work has in the process become more suitable for readers with different social backgrounds. This translation is therefore the fruit of a concerted effort, based on a desire for true benefit, on behalf of the translator, and in addition shows an admirable ability.

I would like to express my appreciation to Venerable Puriso for his wholesome intentions and commitment in translating this work into English, and also setting the manuscript up for printing on computer. I would also like to express my appreciation to Ven. Phramahā Insorn Cintāpañño, who helped to finalise the setting up, and the Buddha Dhamma Foundation, who have taken on the financial responsibility.

May the collected wholesome intentions of all concerned serve to encourage right understanding and right conduct, which are the conditions which will bring about peace and happiness in the world today, in accordance with the author's intentions.

Bhikkhu P.A. Payutto
October 15, 1992 (B.E. 2535)

INTRODUCTION

THE WORK presented here is based on a single chapter from *Buddha Dhamma*, by the Most Venerable Phra Thepvedi Payutto (Bhikkhu P.A. Payutto). *Buddha Dhamma* is perhaps the author's most formal and ambitious book to date, a volume of over one thousand pages dealing with the whole of the Buddha's teaching. The work is scholarly in approach, and yet always tries to simplify the Buddhist themes so often misunderstood or considered beyond the scope of the layman, making them more available on the practical level.

The venerable author is one of the foremost Buddhist scholars in Thailand today. His vast output of material ranges from simple explanations of basic Buddhist themes, to more substantial Dhamma teachings of a commentarial nature (such as *Buddha Dhamma*) and numerous social analyses from a Buddhist perspective. Venerable Thepvedi is unusually gifted in this regard, having had experience of both Eastern and Western cultures in the course of his studies and his teaching career. This, combined with an enquiring mind, exhaustive research, and an intuitive understanding of rare scope, gives the Venerable Ajahn* an outstanding position from which to present the Buddha's teaching.

For the modern Westerner, the teaching of *kamma* offers a path of practice based not on fear of a higher authority, nor dogma, but rather founded on a clear understanding of the natural law of cause and effect as it relates to human behaviour. It is a teaching to be not so much believed in as **understood** and seen in operation.

Buddhism, therefore, is a religion which puts wisdom to the fore rather than faith. Intelligent and honest enquiry are not only

---

* 'Ajahn', the Thai form of the Pali word 'Ācariya', meaning 'teacher', is a commonly used form of address for Thai monks.

welcomed, but encouraged. Part of this enquiry requires a good background understanding of the way cause and effect functions on the personal level. This is the domain of ethics, or moral practice, and is the specific domain of *kamma*. What criteria are there for right and wrong behaviour? As concepts these words are open to a wide range of interpretations, but in the study of *kamma* we are concerned with finding interpretations that are workable and sound. Such a definition must be one which not only points out a clear direction for moral conduct, but also provides the reasons and incentives for maintaining it. The teaching of *kamma* satisfies these requirements.

Western society today lacks clarity or a coherent direction in moral issues. With the rejection of belief in a Supreme Being, or at least the waning of faith that followed the advances of science, all that seems to remain as a prescription for life are political systems and social ideals. When authoritarian rule is rejected, it often means a rejection of any coherent behavioural standard. There seems to be no room in modern thinking for ethics, except perhaps on the level of ideals, such as in the human rights movements and similar appeals to human conscience.

In the age of personal freedom and the right to self-expression, ethics seems to have been reduced to a matter of personal opinion, social decree or cultural preference. Concepts such as 'right' and 'wrong', and 'good' and 'evil', no longer stand on solid ground, and we find ourselves more and more floundering when asked to define them. Are these qualities simply a matter of opinion, or do they have some reality based on the facts of human life? How do they relate to the scientific world of impersonal cause and effect relationships? In the eyes of many, these concepts have been reduced to tools for righteous bigotry or political opportunism. This is why it is irksome for so many people to see or hear the word 'morality'; the subject is a decidedly boring one for most. In an age when life seems to be offering an endless succession of 'cheap thrills', who's interested in restraint?

Even so, without any clear direction in life we are faced with problems on many levels. With no clear direction, no guidelines on which to base life, it becomes a shabby collection of blunders, clumsily groping from one experience to the next – even more so when the meaning of life is reduced to a compulsive race to amass 'experiences' for their own sake. The result is a society driven by hedonism, fueled by desire, and plagued with problems: on the personal level, depression, loneliness, and nervous disorders; on the communal level, irrational behaviour, crime and social unrest. And at the most subtle level, the legacy of the present age is a life out of step with nature, producing the spiritual 'angst' which has led to the modern search for enlightenment from Eastern sources.

It is in the light of precisely this situation that the Law of *Kamma* is so relevant. Although the words *'kamma'*, or *'karma'**, are sometimes heard in the present day, the concept rarely emerges from the cloud of mystery which has enshrouded it from its first introduction to the West. Strangely so, because in fact the Law of *Kamma* is a singularly dynamic and lucid teaching, one which is particularly pertinent to the modern age. In the Law of *Kamma* we are able to find meaningful and relevant definitions of 'good' and 'evil', an understanding of which not only clarifies the path of ethical practice, but also facilitates personal well-being and fulfillment. Not only individual needs, but problems and directions on a social level can be more readily understood with the help of this teaching. It is no wonder, then, that the Law of *Kamma* is one of the cornerstones of Buddhism.

It is my belief that the present book is an invaluable reference for both the casual student and the more committed practicioner of Buddhism. The Law of *Kamma*, as one of Buddhism's central themes, requires not only a modicum of learning, but also a good deal of inner reflection. The book should therefore not be read as simply a collection of ideas to be committed to memory, but as 'food for

---

* Kamma – the Pali spelling, which is used throughout this book, is not as familiar as the Sanskrit spelling, Karma, although they both mean the same.

thought', to be mulled over, reflected on and applied to practical reality. Some of the concepts presented will at first seem strange to many readers, but time spent contemplating them will reveal that these concepts, far from strange, are singularly 'ordinary'. They are in fact the most obvious of truths; and yet they somehow elude our complicated minds.

I originally set out to make a fairly literal translation of this book, but having completed the first draft I was faced with a number of problems. Firstly, many of the points raised in the book were issues which applied specifically to Thai culture and would only be meaningful in such a context. One section, for instance, covered the difference between *kusala* (skilful) and *akusala* (unskilful) on one hand, and *puñña* (merit) and *pāpa* (demerit) on the other, these words being extensively used in Thailand. But they are fairly untranslatable in English. For this reason I asked the venerable author for permission to delete this section. Some sections, such as the section on intention, were moved from one chapter to another. On all of these occasions I have sought out the venerable author's permission and advice.

One of the major changes to the book is the addition of a new chapter, on Social Kamma, which was put together from a tape made of an informal series of questions and answers on the subject between the author and the translator. The subject is in fact a very broad one, one which could be easily expanded into a book in itself. It is also one aspect of *kamma* which is particularly relevant to modern western interests, and for this reason was expanded on and incorporated into this English version.

In general, the nature of the two languages, Thai and English, are vastly different. What is considered good Thai, if rendered directly into English, sometimes turns into bad English. The Thai language is a very relaxed one, preferring to pursue a subject casually, enjoying the sights on the way, so to speak. A few extra words thrown in, plenty of adjectives (often as many as ten different words for each concept, for instance, each with its own tonal effect), and so on lead to what in the English language we might consider to be 'redundancy' or 'long-windedness'. English, on the other hand, a comparatively more impatient language, prefers concise phrases, only one or two adjectives or nouns in one string, and as direct a presentation of the subject as possible. Given this, I was faced with the choice of remaining faithful to the original text at the expense of readability, or acting as editor as well as translator. I have tried to find a good middle way between the two extremes.

There are a number of Pali words which it was felt were better left untranslated in the body of the text, in the hope that some of these words may, in time, find their way into the English language in one form or another. These are words for which the English language has no direct translations, and as such they represent an unfortunate lack for the Western world as a whole.

All in all, the book is by no means a literal translation, as anyone familiar with the two languages will find out. For any shortcomings regarding both the language, the quality of translation, and the amount of editing that has gone into this work, I ask the reader's forgiveness, and can only hope that the shortcomings are surmountable to an earnest student on the quest for truth.

Finally I should mention that the manuscript has been read over by so many people as to be too numerous to mention here. I have relied on the suggestions and feedback of all of them to guide my treatment of the translation, hoping to present the book in as 'universal' a way as possible. May any merits accruing from the production of this book serve to illuminate the subject of *kamma,* and thereby lead to a saner world for all.

Unless otherwise indicated, all footnotes are mine.

The Translator

CONTENTS

1 UNDERSTANDING THE LAW OF KAMMA

Kamma as a law of nature

B UDDHISM TEACHES that all things, both material and immaterial, are entirely subject to the direction of causes, and are inter-dependent. This natural course of things is called in common terms 'the law of nature', and in Pali *niyāma,* literally meaning 'certainty' or 'fixed way', referring to the fact that specific determinants inevitably lead to corresponding results.

These laws of nature, although uniformly based on the principle of causal dependence, can nevertheless be sorted into different modes of relationship. The Buddhist commentaries describe five categories of natural law, or *niyāma.* They are:

1   *UTUNIYĀMA:* the natural law pertaining to physical objects, especially changes in the natural environment, such as weather, winds and rainfall; natural phenomena such as the way flowers bloom in the day and fold up at night; the way soil, water and nutrients help a tree to grow; the way things disintegrate and decompose. This perspective emphasizes the changes brought about by heat or temperature.

2   *BĪJANIYĀMA:* the natural law pertaining to heredity, as in, 'as the seed, so the fruit'.

3   *CITTANIYĀMA:* the natural law pertaining to the workings of the mind, such as the process of cognition of sensations and the mind's reactions to them; the movement of the *bhavaṅga-citta** and so on. These are all governed by *cittaniyāma.*

4   *KAMMANIYĀMA:* the natural law pertaining to human behaviour, that is the process of the generation of action and its

---

* *Bhavaṅga-citta* – The mind in its dormant, inactive state; the subliminal state of mind.

results. Specifically, this refers to the workings of **intention,** or the process of mental proliferation and its consequences. In essence, this is summarised in the words, '**good deeds bring good results, bad deeds bring bad results**'.

5 *DHAMMANIYĀMA:* the natural law governing the relationship and interdependence of all things: that is, the way all things arise, exist and then cease – this is the Norm; all beings experience birth, aging, sickness and death as a normal condition; human beings normally live to less than a hundred years; regardless of whether or not a Buddha arises, all things are as a rule subject to change, are in a state of affliction and are not self. This is the Norm.

The first four *niyāma* are contained within, or derived from, the fifth one, *Dhammaniyāma*, the Law of Dhamma, or the Law of Nature. It may be questioned why *Dhammaniyāma*, being as it were the totality, is included at all within the sub-divisions. It is because *Dhammaniyāma* is not exhausted by this four-fold categorization. For illustration we may refer to a comparison: the population of Thailand, for example, may be sorted into different categories, such as the king, the government, public servants, merchants and the populace; or it may be categorized as the police, military, public servants, students and the populace; or it can be divided up in a number of other ways. Actually, these words 'the populace' include all the other groupings in the country. Public servants, householders, police, the military, merchants and students are all equally members of the populace, but they are singled out because each of those groups has its own unique characteristics. Those people without any relevant feature particular to them are grouped under the general heading, 'the populace'. Moreover, although those groupings may change according to their particular design, they will always include the word 'the populace', or 'the people', or a similar generic term. The inclusion of *Dhammaniyāma* in the five *niyāma* should be understood in this way.

Whether or not these five natural laws are complete and all-inclusive is not important. The commentators have detailed the

tive groupings relevant to their needs, and any other groupings can be included under the fifth one, *Dhammaniyāma,* in the same way as in the example above. The important point to bear in mind is the commentators' design in pointing out these five *niyāma.* In this connection three points should be mentioned:

Firstly, this teaching highlights the Buddhist perspective, seeing the course of things – the world and life of the world – as subject to causes and conditions. No matter how minutely this law is analysed, we see only the workings of the Norm, or the state of inter-dependence. Knowing this allows us to learn, live and prac-tise with a clear and firm understanding of the way things are. We need not concern ourselves over questions of a Creator God with the power to induce the flow of the Norm to deviate (unless that God becomes one of the determining factors within that flow). When challenged with such misleading questions as, "Without a being to create these laws, how can they come to be?", we need only reflect that if left to themselves, all things must function in some way or other, and this is the way they function. It is impossible for them to function any other way. Human beings, observing and studying this state of things, then proceed to call it a 'law'. But whether it is called a law or not does not change its actual operation.

Secondly, in our analysis of this one law of nature, we must by no means reduce events entirely to single laws. In actual fact, one and the same event in nature may arise from any one of these laws, or a combination of them. For example, the blooming of the lotus in the day time and its folding up at night are not the effects of *utuniyāma* (the law of the elements) alone, but are also subject to *bījaniyāma* (heredity). When a human being sheds tears it may be due largely to the effects of *cittaniyāma,* as with happy or sad mental states, or it could be the work of *utuniyāma,* such as from getting smoke in the eyes.

Thirdly, and most importantly, here the commentators are showing us that the law of *kamma,* or *kammaniyāma,* is just one of a number of natural laws. The fact that it is given as only one among five different laws reminds us that we should not immediately write all events off, pleasant or unpleasant, as the workings of *kamma*. We might say that *kamma* is that force which directs society, or decides the values and lives within it. Although it is simply one type of natural law, it is the most important one for human beings, because it is their particular responsibility. Human beings are the instigators of *kamma,* and *kamma* shapes the fortunes and conditions of their lives. Looking at the world as most people tend to do, that is, divided up into the sphere of influence for which nature is responsible, and that for which human beings are responsible, we will see that *kammaniyāma* is a strictly human responsibility. As for the other *niyāma,* they are entirely the domain of nature.

Within the sphere of *kammaniyāma,* the factor of intention or volition is crucial. Thus, *kammaniyāma* is the law which governs the realm of volition, or the world of intentional human thought and action. Whether or not they must deal with other *niyāma,* human beings must deal with *kammaniyāma.* Even their dealings with other *niyāma* are inevitably influenced by *kammaniyāma. Kammaniyāma* is thus a primarily human affair, regulating the extent to which human beings are able to create and control the things around them.

Correctly speaking, we could say that the human capacity to enter into and become one of the factors within the natural cause and effect continuum, which in turn gives rise to the impression that they are able to control and manoeuvre nature, is all due to this *kammaniyāma*. In scientific and technological areas, for example, human beings interact with the other *niyāma,* or natural laws, by studying their truths and acting upon them in accordance with their nature, creating the impression that human beings are able to manipulate and control the natural world.

In addition to this, human beings shape their own social and personal relationships, as well as their interactions with other things and the environment around them, through volition or intention. Through volition, human beings shape themselves and their lifestyles, social positions and fortunes. It is because *kam-maniyāma* is a specifically human concern, covering the entire volitional and creative world of human beings, that the Buddha's teaching greatly stresses its importance. This can be seen in the words: **Kammunā vattatī loko: The world is directed by kamma**[1].

The law of *kamma* and Social Convention.

Apart from the five kinds of natural law mentioned above, there is another kind of law which is specifically man-made and is not directly concerned with nature. These are the codes of law fixed and agreed upon by society, consisting of social decrees, customs, laws and so on. They could be placed at the end of the above list as a sixth kind of law, but they do not have a Pali name. Let's call them Social Convention*. These codes of social law are products of human thought and as such are related to *kammaniyāma*. They are, however, merely a supplement to *kammaniyāma,* they are not *kammaniyāma* as such, and do not have the same relationship with natural truth as does *kammaniyāma,* as will presently be shown. However, because they are found within *kammaniyāma* they tend to become confused with it, and misunderstandings frequently arise as a result. Because these two kinds of laws, *kammaniyāma* and Social Convention, are human concerns and are intimately related to human beings, it is very important that the differences between them are clearly understood.

In general we might state that the law of *kamma* is the **natural law** which deals with human actions, whereas Social Convention, or social law, is an entirely human creation. It is related to nature only insofar as it is a product of the natural human thought process. **In essence, with the law of *kamma*, human**

---

* In the Thai language here the Venerable author makes use of the similarity between these two words, 'gummaniyahm' *(kammaniyāma)* and 'sungkom niyom' (social preference), to give these terms a certain amount of fluency that is lost in the English.

5

beings receive the fruits of their actions according to the natural processes, whereas in social law, human beings take responsibility for their actions via a process established by themselves.

The Meaning of *Kamma*

Etymologically speaking, *kamma* means 'work' or 'action'. But in the context of Dhamma we define it more specifically as 'action based on intention *(cetanā)*' or 'deeds wilfully done'. Actions that are free of intention are not considered to be *kamma* in the Buddha's teaching.

This definition is, however, a very general one. If we wish to clarify it and see its whole range of meaning, we must analyse it more thoroughly, dividing it up into different perspectives, or levels, thus:

a. *Kamma* as intention

Essentially *kamma* is **intention**, which includes volition, will, choice and decision, or the energy which leads to action. Intention is that which instigates and directs all human actions. It is the agent or prompting force in all human creation and destruction, therefore it is the actual essence of *kamma,* as is given in the Buddha's words, **Cetanāhaṁ bhikkhave kammaṁ vadāmi : Bhikkhus! Intention, I say, is *kamma*. Having willed, we create *kamma*, through body, speech and mind.** [2]

At this point we should broaden our understanding of this word 'intention' *(cetanā)*. 'Intention' in the context of Dhamma has a much more subtle meaning than it has in common usage. In the English language, we tend to use the word 'intention' when we want to provide a link between internal thought and its resultant external actions. For example, we tend to say, 'I didn't intend to do it', 'I didn't mean to say it' or 'he did it intentionally'. But according to the teachings of Dhamma, all actions and speech, all thoughts, no matter how fleeting, and the responses of the mind to the various images received through eye, ear, nose, tongue and body, and recollected in the mind itself, without exception, contain elements of intention. Intention is thus the volitional or conscious choosing of objects of awareness by the mind. It is the factor which leads the mind to turn towards, or be repelled from, various objects of awareness or mental concerns, or to proceed in any particular direction. It is the guide, the manager or the governor of how the mind responds to stimuli. It is the force which plans and organizes the movements of the mind, and ultimately it is that which determines the numerous states experienced by the mind.

One instance of intention is one instance of *kamma*. When there is *kamma* there is immediate result. Even just one little thought, although not particularly important, is nevertheless not void of consequence. It will be at the least a 'tiny speck' of *kamma*, accumulating to become an agent for conditioning the qualities of internal mental activity. If it increases, through repeated creation by the mind, or through an increase in intensity, transforming into external activity, the result becomes stronger, expanding to become character traits, physical features or results from external sources.

A destructive intention does not have to be as obvious as one of murder, for example. It may lead to the destruction of only a very small thing, such as when angrily tearing up a piece of paper. Even though that piece of paper may have no importance in itself, the action still has some effect on the quality of the mind. The effect is very different from tearing up a piece of paper with a neutral mental state, such as when throwing out a piece of scrap paper. If there is repeated implementation of such intention, the effects of accumulation will become clearer and clearer, and may extend to higher levels.

Consider the specks of dust which come floating unnoticed into a room: there isn't one speck which is void of consequence. It is the same for the mind. But the weight of that consequence, in addition to being dependent on the amount of 'dust', is also related to the quality and the functioning of the mind on various levels. For instance, specks of dust which alight onto a road surface have to be of a very large quantity before the road will seem to be dirty. Specks of dust which alight onto a floor, although of a much smaller quantity, will already seem dirty. A smaller amount of dust accumulating on a table top will seem dirty enough to cause irritation. An even smaller amount alighting on a mirror will seem dirty and will interfere with its functioning. A tiny speck of dust on a spectacle lens is perceptible and can impair vision. In the same way, volition or intention, no matter how small, is not void of fruit. As the Buddha said:

"All *kamma,* whether good or evil, bears fruit. There is no *kamma,* no matter how small, which is void of fruit."[3]

In any case, the mental results of *kammaniyāma* are overlooked and regarded as unimportant by most people. Therefore another illustration might be helpful:

– There are many levels of clean or dirty water: the dirty water in a sewer, the water in a canal, tap water, and distilled water for mixing a hypodermic injection. Sewer water is an acceptable habitat for many kinds of water animals, but is not suitable for bathing, drinking or any more refined use. Water in a canal may be used to bathe or to wash clothes but is not drinkable. Tap water is drinkable but cannot be used for mixing a hypodermic injection. If there is no special need, then tap water is sufficient for most purposes, but if water was needed to mix with a hypodermic injection, one would be ill-advised to use tap water. This is comparable to the mind with varying levels of refinement or clarity, depending on accumulated *kamma.* As long as the mind is still being used on a coarse level, no problem may be apparent. But as time progresses, there may come a need to use the mind on a more refined level, at which time previous unskilful *kamma* will become an obstacle.

b. *Kamma* **as conditioning factor**

Expanding our perspective, we can see *kamma* as a component within the whole life process, being **the agent which fashions the**

direction taken in life. This is *kamma* in its sense of *'sankhāra*', as it appears in the Wheel of Dependent Origination**, where it is described as the agent which fashions the mind. This refers to the factors or qualities of the mind which, with intention at the lead, shape the mind into good, evil or neutral states, which in turn fashion the thought process and its manifestations through body and speech. In this context, *kamma* could be defined simply as mental proliferation. Even in this definition we still take intention as the essence, and thus we sometimes see *sankhāra* translated simply as intention.

c. *Kamma* as personal responsibility

Now let's look further outward, from the level of the individual in his relation to the world. *Kamma* from this angle refers to the manifestations of thoughts through speech and actions, that is, **behaviour from an ethical perspective,** either on a narrow, immediate level, or on a broader level including the past and the future. *Kamma* in this sense corresponds to the very broad, general meaning given above. This is the meaning of *kamma* which is most often encountered in the scriptures, where it occurs as an inducement to encourage responsible action and the making of good *kamma*, as in the Buddha's words:

"Bhikkhus! These two things are a cause of remorse. What are the two? Some people in this world have not made good *kamma*, have not been skilful, have not made merit as a safeguard against fear. They have committed only bad *kamma*, only coarse *kamma*, only harmful *kamma* ... They experience remorse as a result, thinking, 'I have not made good *kamma*. I have made only bad *kamma*.'"[4] ...

It is worth noting that these days, not only is *kamma* almost always taught from this perspective, but it is also treated largely from the perspective of past lives.

* Determinant
** *Paṭiccasamuppāda*

d. *Kamma* as social activity or career

From an even broader radius, that is, from the perspective of social activity, we have *kamma* in its sense of **work, labour or profession.** This is the conduct of human life and the labours resulting from intention and creative thinking, which in turn affect society, such as can be observed in the present time. As is stated in the *Vāseṭṭha Sutta:*

"Listen, Vāseṭṭha, you should understand it thus: One who depends on farming for a livelihood is a farmer, not a Brahmin; one who makes a living with the arts is an artist ... one who makes a living by selling is a merchant ... one who makes a living working for others is a servant ... one who makes a living through stealing is a thief ... one who makes a living by the knife and the sword is a soldier ... one who makes a living by officiating at religious ceremonies is a priest, not a Brahmin ... one who rules the land is a king, not a Brahmin ... I say that he who has no defilements staining his mind, who is devoid of clinging, is a Brahmin ... One does not become a Brahmin simply by birth, but by *kamma* is one a Brahmin, by *kamma* is one not a Brahmin. By *kamma* is one a farmer, an artist, a merchant, a servant, a thief, a soldier, a priest or even a king ... it is all because of *kamma*. The wise person, seeing Dependent Origination, skilled in *kamma* and *vipāka**, sees *kamma* as it is in this way. The world is directed by *kamma*. Humanity is directed by *kamma* ... "[5]

In any case, having looked at these four different shades of meaning for the word '*kamma*', still it must be stressed that any definition of *kamma* should always be based on **intention.** Intention is the agent which guides our relationships with other things, and is the deciding factor for the direction and style of those relationships. Whether a person will act under the influence of unskilful tendencies, in the form of greed, hatred and delusion, or skilful tendencies, is all entirely at the discretion of intention. Any act which is devoid of

---

* *Vipāka:* The results of *kamma*

10

intention has no bearing on *kammaniyāma*. That is, it does not come into the law of *kamma*, but comes under the domain of one of the other *niyāma*, such as *utuniyāma*. Such actions have the same value as a pile of earth caving in, a rock falling from a mountain, or a dead branch falling from a tree.

Kinds of *kamma*

In terms of its qualities, or its roots, *kamma* can be divided into two main types. They are:

1. Akusala kamma: kamma which is unskilful, actions which are not good, or are evil; specifically, actions which are born from the *akusala mūla,* the roots of unskilfulness, which are greed, hatred and delusion*.

2. Kusala kamma: kamma which is skilful or skilful action; specifically, actions which are born from the three *kusala mūla,* or roots of skill, which are non-greed, non-hatred and non-delusion.

Alternatively *kamma* can be classified according to the paths or channels through which it occurs, of which there are three. They are:

**1. Bodily *kamma:* *kamma* through the body.

**2. Verbal *kamma:* *kamma* through speech.

**3. Mental *kamma:* *kamma* through the mind.

Incorporating both of the classifications described above, we have altogether six kinds of *kamma:* bodily, verbal and mental *kamma* which is unskilful; and bodily, verbal and mental *kamma* which is skilful.

Another way of classifying *kamma* is according to its results. In this classification there are four categories:

1. Black *kamma,* black result: This refers to bodily actions, verbal actions and mental actions which are harmful. Simple examples are killing, stealing, sexual infidelity, lying and drinking intoxicants**.

---

* *Lobha, dosa* and *moha.*

** These are the practices proscribed by the Five Precepts, the basic moral standard for a practising Buddhist.

11

2. White *kamma*, white result: These are bodily actions, verbal actions and mental actions which are not harmful, such as practising in accordance with the ten bases for skilful action*

3.*Kamma* that is both black and white, giving results both black and white: Bodily actions, verbal actions and mental actions which are partly harmful, partly not, such as the actions of people generally.

4. *Kamma* which is neither black nor white, results neither black nor white, leading to the cessation of *kamma*. This is the intention to transcend the three kinds of *kamma* mentioned above, or specifically, developing the Seven Enlightenment Factors or the Noble Eight-fold Path**.

Of those three types of *kamma*, bodily, verbal and mental, it is mental *kamma* which is considered the most important and far-reaching in its effects, as is given in the Pali:

"Listen, Tapassi. Of these three types of *kamma* so distinguished by me, I say that mental *kamma* has the heaviest consequences for the committing of evil deeds, for the existence of evil deeds, not bodily or verbal *kamma*."[6]

Mental *kamma* is considered to be the most significant because it is the origin of all other *kamma*. Thought precedes action through body and speech. Verbal and bodily actions are therefore derived from mental *kamma*.

One of the most important factors of mental *kamma* is *diṭṭhi*, which includes beliefs, views, theories, and personal preferences. *Diṭṭhi* is that which colours individual behaviour, life experiences and social ideals. With beliefs, opinions or preferences as a base,

---

** The ten bases of skilful action: Refraining from killing, stealing, sexual misconduct, lying, malicious tale-bearing, abusive speech, frivolous speech, covetousness, ill will and wrong view.
*** The Noble Eight-fold Path: Right View, Right Intention, Right Speech, Right Action, Right Livelihood, Right Effort, Right Recollection and Right Concentration. The Seven Factors of Enlightenment: Recollection, Inquiry into Dhamma, Effort, Rapture, Tranquillity, Concentration and Equanimity.

there follow the manoeuvring, speech and actions in accordance with those beliefs. If there is wrong view, it follows that the consequent thinking, speech and actions will also tend to flow in a wrong direction. If there is right view, then the resultant thoughts, speech and actions will tend to flow in a proper and good direction. This applies not only to the personal level, but to the social level as well. For example, a society which maintained the belief that material wealth is the most valuable and desirable goal in life would strive to attain material possessions, gauging progress, prestige and honour by abundance of these things. The lifestyle of such people and the direction such a society took would assume one form. In contrast, a society and people which valued peace and contentment of mind as its goal would have a correspondingly different lifestyle and direction.

There are many occasions where the Buddha described right view, wrong view, and their importance, such as:

"Bhikkhus! **What is Right View? I say that there are two kinds of Right View: the Right View (of one) with *āsava** (*lokiya sammādiṭṭhi,* or worldly Right View), which is good *kamma* and of beneficial result to the *khandhas***; and the Right View (of one) without *āsava*, which is transcendent (*Lokuttara*), and is a factor of the (Noble) Path.**

"And what is the Right View which contains *āsava*, which is good and of beneficial result to the *khandhas?* This is the belief that offerings bear fruit, the practice of giving bears fruit, reverence is of fruit, good and evil *kamma* give appropriate results; there is this world, there is an after-world; there is a mother, there is a father; there are spontaneously arisen beings; there are mendicants and religious who practise well and who proclaim clearly the truths of this world and the next. This

---

* *Āsava:* Literally, 'taints', or 'outflows'. These are the deep-seated roots of defilements, three and sometimes four in number:Sensual desire, desire for becoming, attachment to views and ignorance.
** The Five *Khandhas:* Form, or body, feeling, perception, volitional activities and consciousness – or, in short, body and mind.

I call the Right View which contains the *āsava*, which is good, and is of beneficial result to the *khandhas* ..."[7]

"*Bhikkhus!* I see no other condition which is so much a cause for the arising of as yet unarisen unskilful conditions, and for the development and fruition of unskilful conditions already arisen, as wrong view ..."[8]

"*Bhikkhus!* I see no other condition which is so much a cause for the arising of as yet unarisen skilful conditions, and for the development and fruition of skilful conditions already arisen, as right view ..."[8]

"*Bhikkhus!* When there is wrong view, bodily *kamma* created as a result of that view, verbal *kamma* created as a result of that view, and mental *kamma* created as a result of that view, as well as intentions, aspirations, wishes and mental proliferations, are all productive of results that are undesirable, unpleasant, disagreeable, yielding no benefit, but conducive to suffering. On what account? On account of that pernicious view. It is like a margosa seed, or a seed of the bitter gourd, planted in moist earth. The soil and water taken in as nutriment are wholly converted into a bitter taste, an acrid taste, a foul taste. Why is that? Because the seed is not good.

"*Bhikkhus!* When there is right view, bodily *kamma* created as a result of that view, verbal *kamma* created as a result of that view, and mental *kamma* created as a result of that view, as well as intentions, aspirations, wishes and mental proliferations, are all yielding of results that are desirable, pleasant, agreeable, producing benefit, conducive to happiness. On what account? On account of those good views. It is like a seed of the sugar cane, a seed of wheat, or a fruit seed which has been planted in moist earth. The water and soil taken in as nutriment are wholly converted into sweetness, into refreshment, into a delicious taste. On what account is that? On account of that good seed ..."[9]

"*Bhikkhus!* There is one whose birth into this world is not for the benefit of the many, not for the happiness of the many, but for the ruin, for the harm of the manyfolk, for the suffering of both devas and men. Who is that person? It is the person with wrong view, with distorted views. One with wrong view leads the many away from the truth and into falsehood...

"Bhikkhus! There is one whose birth into this world is for the benefit of the many, for the happiness of the many, for growth, for benefit, for the happiness of devas and men. Who is that person? It is the person with right view, who has undistorted views. One with right view leads the many away from falsehood, and toward the truth ..."

"Bhikkhus! I see no other condition which is so harmful as wrong view. Of harmful things, *bhikkhus,* wrong view is the greatest."[10]

"All conditions have mind as forerunner, mind as master, are accomplished by mind. With a defective mind, whatever one says or does brings suffering in its wake, just as the cart-wheel follows the ox's hoof ... With a clear mind, whatever one says or does brings happiness in its wake, just as the shadow follows its owner."[11]

2 ON GOOD AND EVIL

The Problem of Good and Evil

BECAUSE *kamma* is directly concerned with good and evil, any discussion of *kamma* must also include a discussion of good and evil. Standards for defining good and evil are, however, not without their problems. What is 'good', and how is it so? What is it that we call 'evil', and how is that so? These problems are in fact a matter of language. When it comes to Dhamma, where the Pali language is used, the meaning becomes much clearer, as will presently be demonstrated.

The words 'good' and 'evil' in English* have very broad meanings, particularly the word 'good', which is much more widely used than 'evil'. A virtuous and moral person is said to be good; delicious food might be called good food; a block of wood which happens to be useful might be called a good block of wood. In the same way, something which is said by one person to be good might not be good to many others. Looked at from one angle a certain thing may be good, but not from another. Behaviour which is considered good in one area, district or society might not be so in another.

It can be seen from these examples that there is some disparity. It might be necessary to consider the word 'good' from different viewpoints, such as 'good' in a hedonistic sense, 'good' in an artistic sense, 'good' in an economic sense, and so on. The reason for this disparity is a matter of what we call 'values'. The words 'good' and 'bad' can be used in all value systems in English, which makes their

---

*In the original version of course, the word here would be 'Thai', but 'English' seems to apply just as well.

meanings very broad and unclear. In the hope of avoiding confusion, then, the words 'good' and 'evil' as they are used in English will not be used here.

In our study of 'good' and 'evil' the following points should be born in mind:

a. Our investigation of good and evil here will be from the perspective of the law of *kamma,* thus we will be using the specialized terms *'kusala'* and *'akusala'* or skilful and unskilful. These two words have very precise meanings.

b. *Kusala* and *akusala,* in terms of Buddhist ethics, are aspects of the law of *kamma,* thus our study of them is keyed to this context, not as a set of social values as commonly implied by the words 'good' and 'bad'.

c. As discussed in Chapter One, the operation of the law of *kamma* is also related to other laws. Specifically, insofar as the inner life of the individual is concerned, *kammaniyāma* interacts with *cittaniyāma* (psychological laws), while externally it is related to Social Convention.

The meaning of *kusala* and *akusala*

Although *kusala* and *akusala* are sometimes translated as 'good' and 'evil', this may be misleading. Things which are *kusala* may not always be considered good, while some things may be *akusala* and yet not generally considered to be evil. Depression, melancholy, sloth and distraction, for example, although *akusala,* are not usually considered to be 'evil' as we know it in English. In the same vein, some forms of *kusala,* such as calmness of body and mind, may not readily come into the general understanding of the English word 'good'. Thus *kusala* and *akusala* and 'good' and 'evil' are not necessarily the same things.

Kusala and akusala are conditions which arise in the mind, producing results initially in the mind, and from there to external actions and physical features. The meanings of *kusala* and *akusala* therefore stress the state, the contents and the events of mind as their basis.

Kusala can be rendered literally as 'intelligent, skilful, content, beneficial, good', or 'that which removes affliction'. *Akusala* is defined in the opposite way, as in 'unintelligent', 'unskilful' and so on.

The following are four connotations of *kusala* derived from the commentaries:

1. *ĀROGYA:* free of illness; that is, the mind free of illness, much as is generally known as 'a healthy mind', referring to those conditions or factors which support mental health, producing a healthy, untroubled and stable mind.

2. *ANAVAJJA:* unstained; the mind that is not stained or murky, but clean, polished and clear.

3. *KOSALASAMBHŪTA:* based on wisdom or intelligence; the quality of mind which contains wisdom, or the various qualities which arise from knowledge and understanding of truth. This corresponds with the teaching which states that *kusala* conditions have *yoniso-manasikāra*, clear thinking, as forerunner.

4. *SUKHAVIPĀKA:* rewarded by well-being. *Kusala* is a condition which produces contentment. When *kusala* conditions arise in the mind there is naturally a sense of well-being, without the need for any external influence. Just as when one is strong and healthy *(āroga)*, freshly bathed *(anavajja)*, and in a safe and comfortable place *(kosalasambhūta)*, a sense of well-being naturally follows.

The meaning of *akusala* should be understood in just the opposite way from above: as the mind that is unhealthy, harmful, based on ignorance, and resulting in suffering. This could be briefly defined as 'those conditions which cause the mind to degenerate, both in quality and efficiency', unlike *kusala*, which promotes the quality and efficiency of the mind.

In order to further clarify these concepts, it might be useful to describe the attributes of a good mind, one that is healthy and trouble-free, and then to consider whether *kusala* conditions do indeed induce the mind to be this way, and if so, how. We could then consider whether *akusala* conditions do indeed deprive the mind of such states, and how they do this.

For easy reference, we could compile the various characteristics into groups, like this:

1. **Firm** *(Samāhita)*: resolute, stable, consistent, unmoving, undistracted, unwavering.

2. **Pure** *(Parisuddha)* **and clean** *(Pariyodāta)*: spotless, unstained, immaculate, bright, luminous.

3. **Clear** *(Pabhassara)* **and free** *(Serī)*: unencumbered, unrestricted, free, aloof, exalted, boundless.

4. **Fit for work** *(Kammaniya)*: pliant, gentle, light, fluent, patient, honest, unbiased, sincere.

5. **Calm** *(Santa)* **and content** *(Sukha)*: relaxed, serene, untroubled, not desirous or in want, satisfied.

Having looked at the qualities of a healthy mind, we can now consider the qualities which are known as *kusala* and *akusala*, assessing to see whether they really do affect the quality of the mind and how.

Some examples of *kusala* conditions are: *sati*, recollection, the ability to maintain the attention with whatever object or duty the mind is engaged; *mettā*, love, goodwill; *alobha*, non-greed, absence of desire and attachment (this includes altruistic thoughts); *paññā*, clear understanding of the way things are; *passaddhi*, calm, relaxation and peace; *kusalachanda*, contentment with the good; a desire to know and act in accordance with the truth; *muditā*, joy at the good fortune of others.

Examples of *akusala* conditions are: *kāmachanda*, desire for sensual pleasure; *byāpāda*, ill will; *thīna middha*, dejection, sloth and torpor; *uddhaccakukkucca*, restlessness and anxiety; *vicikicchā*, doubt; *kodha*, anger; *issā*, jealousy; *macchariya*, avarice.

When there is goodwill, *mettā*, the mind is naturally happy, cheerful, and clear. This is a condition which is beneficial to the psyche, supporting the quality and efficiency of the mind. Goodwill is therefore *kusala*. *Sati* enables the attention to be with whatever the mind is involved or engaged, recollecting the proper course of action, helping to prevent *akusala* conditions from arising, and thus enabling the mind to work more effectively. *Sati* is therefore *kusala*.

Jealousy *(issā)* oppresses the mind and makes it spiteful, clearly damaging the quality and health of the mind. Jealousy is therefore *akusala*. Anger *(kodha)* agitates the mind in such a way that rapidly affects even the health of the body. It can thus be clearly seen as *akusala*. Sensual desire *(kāmachanda)* confuses and obsesses the mind. This is also *akusala*.

Having established an understanding of the words *kusala* and *akusala,* we are now ready to understand good and bad *kamma,* or *kusala kamma* and *akusala kamma*. As has been already mentioned, *cetanā,* or intention, is the heart of *kamma*. Thus, an intention which comprises *kusala* is *kusala cetanā,* (skilful intention) or *kusala kamma* (skilful action). An intention which contains *akusala* is *akusala cetanā* (unskilful intention) or *akusala kamma* (unskilful action). When those skilful or unskilful intentions manifest through the body (bodily actions), speech or mind, they are known as skilful and unskilful *kamma* through body, speech and mind respectively, or, alternatively, bodily *kamma,* verbal *kamma* and mental *kamma* which are skilful and unskilful respectively.

Kusala and *akusala* as catalysts for each other

An act of faith or generosity, moral purity, or even experience of insight during meditation, which are all *kusala* conditions, can precipitate the arising of conceit, pride and arrogance. Conceit and pride are *akusala* conditions. This situation is known as 'kusala as an agent for *akusala*'. Meditation, developed to the level of the *jhāna* *

---

* *Jhāna* are the states of unwavering concentration usually referred to as the 'absorption states'.

states *(kusala),* can lead to attachment *(akusala).* The practice of *mettā (kusala),* thoughts of good will and benevolence to others, can, in the presence of a desirable object, precipitate the arising of lust *(akusala).* These are examples of *kusala* becoming an agent for *akusala.*

Sometimes the practice of Dhamma *(kusala)* can be based on a desire to be reborn in heaven *(rāga, akusala).* A child's good behaviour and discipline *(kusala)* can be based on a desire to show off to its elders *(akusala)*; a student's zeal in learning *(kusala)* can stem from ambition *(akusala)*; anger *(akusala),* seen in the light of its harmful effects, can lead to wise reflection and forgiveness *(kusala)*; the fear of death *(akusala)* can encourage self-reflection *(kusala):* these are all examples of *akusala* as an agent for *kusala.*

A young teenager, being warned by his parents not to associate indiscriminately with others, takes no notice and is tempted into drug addiction by his friends. On realizing his situation, he is at once angered and depressed. Remembering his parents' warnings, he may be moved by their compassion *(akusala as an agent for kusala),* but this in turn may merely aggravate his own self-hatred *(kusala as an agent for akusala).*

These changes from *kusala* to *akusala,* or *akusala* to *kusala,* occur so rapidly that the untrained mind is usually unable to see them.

Gauging good and bad *kamma*

As has been mentioned above, the law of *kamma* has a very intimate relationship with both *cittaniyāma* (psychological laws) and Social Convention. This very closeness of meaning can easily create misunderstandings. The law of *kamma* is so closely related to *cittaniyāma* that they seem to be one and the same thing, but there is a clear dividing line between the two, and that is, *cetanā* (intention). This is the essence and motivating force of the law of *kamma* and is that which gives the law of *kamma* its distinct niche among the other *niyāma* or laws. *Cittaniyāma,* on the other hand, governs all mental activity, including the unintentional.

The law of *kamma* gives human beings a role to play distinct from the other *niyāma*, allowing them to create their own volitional world (giving rise to the delusion that they are independent of the natural world). Intention must rely on the mechanics of *cittaniyāma* in order to function, and the process of creating *kamma* must operate within the parameters of *cittaniyāma*.

Using the analogy of a man driving a motor boat, the 'driver' is intention, which is the domain of the law of *kamma*, whereas the whole of the boat engine is comparable to the numerous mental factors, which are functions of *cittaniyāma*. The driver must depend on the boat engine. However, for the 'boat engine' to lead the 'boat', that is, life and the body, in any direction, is entirely at the discretion of the 'driver', intention. The driver depends on and makes use of the boat, but also takes responsibility for the welfare of both boat and engine. In the same way, the law of *kamma* depends on and makes use of *cittaniyāma*, and is also responsible for the welfare of life, including both the body and the mind.

There is not much confusion about this relationship between the law of *kamma* and *cittaniyāma*, because these are not things in which the average person takes much interest. The issue that creates the most doubt is the relationship between the law of *kamma* and Social Convention. Ambiguity arises in regard to the nature of good and evil, giving rise to questions such as, 'What is good?', 'What is evil?', 'What is the standard for deciding between good and evil?'.

We often hear people say that good and evil are human or social inventions. One action in one society, time or place, may be said to be good, but in another time and place may be said to be not good. One kind of action may be acceptable to one society, but not in another. Some religions teach that to kill animals for food is not bad, while others teach that to harm beings of any kind is never good. Some societies hold that a child should show respect to its elders and that to argue with them is bad manners, while other societies hold that respect is not dependent on age, and that all people should have the right to express their opinions.

To say that good and evil are matters of human preference and social decree is true to some extent. Even so, the good and evil of Social Convention do not affect or upset the workings of the law of *kamma* in any way, and should not be confused with it. 'Good' and 'evil' as social conventions should be recognized as Social Convention. As for 'good' and 'evil', or more correctly, *kusala* and *akusala*, as qualities of the law of *kamma,* these should be recognized as attributes of the law of *kamma*. Even though the two are related they are in fact separate things, and have very clear distinctions.

That which is at once the relationship, and the point of difference, between this natural law and the Social Convention is intention, or will. As to how this is so, let us now consider.

Looked at in terms of the law of *kamma,* the conventions of society may be divided into two types:

1) Those which have no direct relationship to *kusala* and *akusala* as found in the *kammaniyāma*.

2) Those which are related to *kusala* and *akusala*.

As for those conventions which have no direct relationship to *kusala* and *akusala*, these are established by society for a specific social function, such as to enable people to live together harmoniously, and they take the form of accepted values or agreements. They may indeed be instruments for creating social peace and harmony, or they may not. They may indeed be useful to society or they may in fact be harmful. All this depends on whether or not those conventions are established with sufficient understanding and wisdom, and whether or not the authority who established them is acting with pure intention.

These kinds of conventions may take many forms – traditions, customs or laws. 'Good' and 'evil' in this respect are strictly matters of Social Convention. They may change in many ways, but their changes are not functions of the law of *kamma,* and must not be confused with them. If a person disobeys these conventions and

23

is punished by society, that is also a matter of Social Convention, not the law of *kamma*.*

Now, let us consider an area in which these social conventions may overlap with the domain of the law of *kamma,* such as when one member of a society refuses to conform to one of its conventions, or infringes it**. In so doing, that person will be acting on a certain intention. This intention is the first step in, and is therefore a concern of, the law of *kamma*. In many societies there will be an attempt to search out this intention for consideration in the judgement of that infringement. That is again a concern of Social Convention, indicating that that particular society is wise and knows how to utilize the law of *kamma*. It is not, however, a function of the law of *kamma* as such.

As for the particular role of the law of *kamma*, regardless of whether society investigates the intention or not, or even whether society is aware of the infringement or not, the law of *kamma* begins to operate simultaneously with the response to the intention which produced that infringement. The process of fruition has already been set in motion, and the instigator begins to experience the fruits of *kamma* from that moment on.

Simply speaking, the deciding factor in the law of *kamma* is whether the intention is *kusala* or *akusala*. In most cases, not to conform with any social convention can only be said to constitute no intentional infringement when society agrees to abandon or to reform that convention. Only then will there be no violation of the public agreement.

This can be illustrated by a simple example. Suppose two people decide to live together. In order to render their lives together as smooth and as convenient as possible, they agree to establish a set of regulations. For example, although working in different places and returning from work at different times, they

---

* Examples of such conventions might be social codes of dress. For instance, before entering a religious building in Thailand it is appropriate to remove shoes and hat, whereas to enter a Christian church it is usually required to wear both.

** – such as by refusing to remove his shoes in a Thai temple.

decide to have the evening meal together. As it would be impractical to wait for each other indefinitely, they agree that each of them should not eat before seven pm. Of those two people, one likes cats and doesn't like dogs, while the other likes dogs and doesn't like cats. For mutual harmony they agree not to bring any pets into the house at all.

Having agreed on these regulations, if either of those two people acts in contradiction to them, there is a case of intentional infringement, and *kamma* arises in accordance with the law of *kamma,* even though, in fact, to eat food before seven pm., or to bring pets into a house, are not in themselves good or evil. Another couple might even establish regulations which are directly opposite to these. And in the event of one of them eventually considering their regulations as no longer tending to their mutual benefit, that person should discuss the matter with the other and together they should reach an agreement. Only then could any intentional nonconformity on that person's part be free of kammic result. This is the distinction between 'good' and 'evil', and 'right' and 'wrong', as changing social conventions, as opposed to the unchanging properties of the law of *kamma, kusala* and *akusala.*

The conventions which are related to *kusala* and *akusala* in the *kammaniyāma* are those conventions established by society which are either *kusala* or *akusala* in accordance with the *kammaniyāma.* Society may or may not make these regulations with a clear understanding of *kusala* and *akusala.* However, regardless of how the society establishes its conventions, the process of *kammaniyāma* continues along its natural course. It does not change along with those social conventions.

For example, in one society it might be acceptable to imbibe intoxicants and addictive drugs. Extreme emotions may be encouraged, and the citizens may be incited to be ambitious and aggressive, so that society will prosper materially. Or it might be generally believed that to kill people of other societies, or, on a lesser scale, to kill animals, is not blameworthy.

25

These are examples where the good and evil of Social Convention and the *kusala* and *akusala* of *kammaniyāma* are at odds with each other. Looked at from a social perspective, those conventions or attitudes may cause both positive or negative results. For example, although a life of tension, ambition and competitiveness may cause a high suicide rate, an unusually large amount of mental and social problems, heart disease and so on, that society may experience rapid material progress. The various events which arise in a society in such a way can often be traced down to *kammaniyāma**.

Social Convention and *kammaniyāma* remain separate and distinct. The fruits of *kamma* proceed according to their own law, independent of such conventions of society which are at odds with it as mentioned above. However, because the convention and the law are related, correct practice in regard to the *kammaniyāma,* that is, actions that are *kusala,* might still give rise to problems on the social level. For example, an abstainer living in a society which approves intoxicating drugs receives the fruits of *kamma* dictated by the law of *kamma.* He doesn't experience the loss of health and mental clarity due to intoxicating drugs, it's true, but in the context of Social Convention, as opposed to the *kammaniyāma,* he may be ridiculed and scorned. And even within the *kammaniyāma* there may arise problems from his intentional opposition to this Social Convention, in the form of mental stress, more or less depending on his wisdom in letting go of the reactions from society.

A progressive society with wise administrators uses the experience accumulated from previous generations in laying down the conventions and laws of society. These become the good and evil of Social Convention, and ideally should be harmonious with the *kusala* and *akusala* of *kammaniyāma*. **The ability to establish a social convention in conformity with the law of *kamma* would seem to be a sound gauge for determining the true extent of a**

---

* See Chapter Four

society's progress or civilization.

In this context, when it is necessary to appraise any convention in the light of good and evil, it would best be considered from two levels. Firstly, in terms of Social Convention, by determining whether or not it has a beneficial result to society. Secondly, in terms of the law of *kamma,* determining whether it is *kusala* or not, whether or not it is beneficial to the human psyche.

Some conventions, even though maintained by societies for long periods of time, are in fact not at all useful to them, even from the point of view of Social Convention, let alone from the point of view of the law of *kamma.* Such societies should agree to abandon those conventions, or it may be necessary for a wise being with pure heart to encourage them to do so*.

In the case of a convention which is seen to be helpful to society and to human progress, but which is not in conformity with the *kusala* of the law of *kamma,* such as one which enhances material progress at the expense of the quality of life, it might be worth considering to see whether the people of that society have not gone astray and mistaken that which is actually not beneficial as being beneficial. A truly beneficial custom should conform with both Social Convention and the law of *kamma.* In other words, it should be beneficial to both the individual and society as a whole.

In this regard we can take a lesson from the situation of society in the present time. Human beings, aspiring to material wealth, holding the view that wealth of material possessions is the path to true happiness, have proceeded to throw their energies into material development. In the process they have wreaked destruction and untold damage on the environment. Now it has become apparent that many such actions were harmful. Even though society appears to be prosperous, humanity has created many new physical dangers, threatening the environment on a global scale.

---

* A case in point would be the caste system in India, which is useful neither from a social, perspective, nor an ethical one. The Buddha pointed out the fallacy of the caste system in the process of teaching the Dhamma.

In the same way as material progress should not be destructive to the physical body, social progress should not be destructive to the clarity of the mind.

The Buddha gave a set of reflections on *kusala* and *akusala* for assessing the nature of good and evil on a practical level, encouraging reflection on the good and evil within (conscience)', together with the teachings of wise beings (these two being the foundation of *hiri ottappa*)*. Thirdly, he recommended pondering the fruits of actions, both individually and on a social basis. Because the nature of *kusala* and *akusala* may not always be clear, the Buddha advised bearing the teachings of the wise in mind. If such teachings are not clear enough, to look at the results of actions, even if only from social considerations. For most people, these three bases for reflection (i.e., individually, socially, and from the pronouncements of sages) can be used to assess behaviour on a number of different levels, ensuring that their actions are as circumspect as possible.

To sum up, the criteria for assessing good and evil are: in the context of whether an action is *kamma* or not, to take intention as the deciding factor; and in the context of whether that *kamma* is good or evil, to consider the matter against these following principles:

Primary Factors
– Enquiring into the roots of actions, whether the intentions for them arose from one of the skilful roots of non-greed, non-aversion or non-delusion, or whether from one of the unskilful roots of greed, aversion or delusion.
– Enquiring into the effects on the psyche, or mental well-being: whether actions render the mind clear, calm and healthy; whether they promote or inhibit the quality of the mind; whether

---

* *Hiri* – sense of shame; *Ottappa* – fear of wrong-doing. *Hiri* and *ottappa* are positive states of mind which lay a foundation for clear conscience and moral integrity. Restraint is natural because of a clear perception of cause and effect.

they encourage the arising of skilful conditions *(kusala)* and the decrease of unskilful conditions, or *vice versa.*

Secondary Factors

1. Considering the quality of one's actions, whether they be open to censure by oneself or not (conscience).

2. Considering the quality of one's actions in terms of the words of the wise.

3. Considering the quality and fruit of those actions
   – towards oneself
   – towards others.

It is possible to classify these standards in a different way, if we clarify two points. First, looking at actions either in terms of their roots, or as *kusala* and *akusala* themselves, are essentially the same thing. Secondly, in regard to approval or censure by the wise, we can say that such wise opinions are generally preserved in our religions, traditions, laws and so on. Even though these conventions are not always wise, and thus any practice which conflicts with them is not necessarily censurable by the wise, still it can be said that such cases are the exception rather than the rule.

We are now ready to summarize our standards for good and evil, or good and bad *kamma,* both strictly according to the law of *kamma* and also in relation to Social Convention, both on an intrinsically moral level and on a socially prescribed one.

1. In terms of direct benefit or harm, by asking: are these actions beneficial to life and the mind? Do they contribute to the quality of life? Do they cause *kusala* and *akusala* conditions to increase or wane?

2. In terms of beneficial or harmful consequences: Are they harmful or conducive of benefit to oneself?

3. In terms of benefit or harm to society: Are they harmful to others, or helpful to them?

4. In terms of conscience, the natural human reflexive capacity: will that *kamma* be open to censure to oneself or not?

5. In terms of social standards: What is the position of

actions in relation to those religious conventions, traditions and customs, including such social institutions as law and so on, which are based on wise reflection (as opposed to those which are simply superstitious or mistaken beliefs)?

Prior to addressing the question of the results of *kamma* in the next chapter, it would be pertinent to consider some of the points described above in the light of the Pali Canon.

"What are skilful *(kusala)* conditions? They are the three roots of skilfulness – non-greed, non-aversion and non-delusion; feelings, perceptions, proliferations and consciousness which contain those roots of skilfulness; bodily *kamma*, verbal *kamma* and mental *kamma* which have those roots as their base: these are skilful conditions."

"What are unskilful *(akusala)* conditions? They are the three roots of unskilfulness – greed, aversion and delusion – and all the defilements which arise from them; feelings, perceptions, proliferations and consciousness which contain those roots of unskilfulness; bodily *kamma*, verbal *kamma* and mental *kamma* which have those roots of unskilfulness as a foundation: these are unskilful conditions." [12]

"There are two kinds of danger, the overt danger and the covert danger.

"What are the 'overt dangers'? These are such things as lions, tigers, panthers, bears, leopards, wolves ... bandits ... eye diseases, ear diseases, nose diseases ... cold, heat, hunger, thirst, defecation, urination, contact with gadflies, mosquitoes, wind, sun, and crawling animals: these are called 'overt dangers'.

"What are the 'covert dangers'? They are bad bodily actions, bad verbal actions, bad mental actions; the hindrances of sensual desire, ill will, sloth and torpor, restlessness and doubt; greed, aversion and delusion; anger, revenge, spite, arrogance, jealousy, meanness, deception, boastfulness, stubbornness, competitiveness, pride, scornfulness, delusion, heedlessness; the defilements, the bad habits; the confusion; the lust; the agitation; all the proliferations that are unskilful: these are the 'covert dangers'.

"They are called 'dangers' for what reason? They are called dangers because they overwhelm, because they cause decline, because they are a shelter.

"They are called dangers because they overwhelm. For what reason? Because those dangers suppress, constrict, overcome, oppress, harass and crush that person...

"They are called dangers because they cause decline. For what reason? Because those dangers bring about the decline of skilful conditions ...

"They are called dangers because they are a shelter. For what reason? Because base, unskilful conditions are born from those things and take shelter within, just as an animal which lives in a hole takes shelter in a hole, a water animal takes shelter in water, or a tree-dwelling animal takes shelter in trees ..." [13]

"When greed, aversion and delusion arise within his mind, they destroy the evil doer, just as the bamboo flower signals the ruin of the bamboo plant ..." [14]

"See here, Your Majesty. These three things, arisen in the world, are not for welfare or benefit, but for woe, for discomfort. What are those three? They are greed, aversion and delusion..." [15]

"*Bhikkhus*, there are these three roots of unskilfulness. What are the three? They are the greed-root, the aversion-root and the delusion-root of unskilfulness ...

"Greed itself is unskilful; whatever *kamma* is created on account of greed, through action, speech or thought, is also unskilful. One in the power of greed, sunk in greed, whose mind is distorted by greed, causes trouble for others by striking them, resenting them, destroying them, censuring them, and banishing them, thinking, 'I am powerful, I am mighty'. That is also unskilful. These many kinds of coarse, unskilful conditions, arising from greed, having greed as their cause, having greed as their source, having greed as condition, persecute the evil doer.

"Hatred itself is unskilful; whatever *kamma* is created on account of hatred, through action, speech or thought, is also unskilful. One in the power of hatred ... causes trouble for others ... that is also unskilful. These many kinds of coarse, unskilful conditions persecute the evil doer...

"Delusion itself is unskilful; whatever *kamma* is created on account of delusion, through action, speech or thought, is also unskilful. One in the power of delusion causes trouble for others ... that is also unskilful. These many kinds of unskilful conditions persecute the evil doer in this way.

"One who is thus caught up, whose mind is thus infected, in the coarse, unskilful conditions born of greed, hatred and delusion, experiences suffering, stress, agitation and anxiety in this present time. At death, at the breaking up of the body, he can expect a woeful bourn, just like a tree which is entwined to its top with a banyan creeper comes to ruin, to destruction, to decline, to dissolution ...

"*Bhikkhus!* There are these three roots of skilfulness. What are the three? They are the non-greed root, the non-aversion root and the non-delusion root ..." [16]

"*Bhikkhus!* There are three root causes of *kamma*. What are the three? They are greed ... hatred ... delusion ...

"Whatever *kamma* is performed out of greed ... hatred ... delusion, is born from greed ... hatred ... delusion, has greed ... hatred ... delusion as its root and as its cause, that *kamma* is unskilful, that *kamma* is harmful, that *kamma* has suffering as a result, that *kamma* brings about the creation of more *kamma*, not the cessation of *kamma*.

"*Bhikkhus!* There are these three root causes of *kamma*. What are the three? They are non-greed ... non-hatred ... non-delusion ...

"Whatever *kamma* is performed out of non-greed ... non-hatred ... non-delusion, is born of non-greed ... non-hatred ... non-delusion, has non-greed ... non-hatred ... non-delusion as its root and its cause, that *kamma* is skilful, that *kamma* is not harmful, that *kamma* has happiness as a result, that *kamma* brings about the cessation of *kamma*, not the creation of more *kamma* ..."[17]

"Listen, *Kālāmas*. When you know for yourselves that these things are unskilful, these things are harmful, these things are censured by the wise, these things, if acted upon, will bring about what is neither beneficial nor conducive to welfare, but will cause suffering, then you should abandon those things."

"Listen, *Kālāmas*. How do you consider this matter? Do greed ... hatred ... delusion in a person, bring about benefit or non-benefit?"

(Answer: Non-benefit, Venerable Sir.)

"One who is desirous ... is angry ... is deluded; who is overwhelmed by greed ... hatred ... delusion, whose mind is thus distorted, as a result resorts to murder, to theft, to adultery, to lying, and encourages others to do so. This is for their non-benefit and non-welfare for a long time to come."

(Answer: That is true, Venerable Sir.)

"Listen, *Kālāmas*. How say you, are those things skilful or unskilful?"

(Answer: They are unskilful, Venerable Sir.)

"Are they harmful or not harmful?"

(Answer: Harmful, Venerable Sir.)

"Praised by the wise, or censured?"

(Answer: Censured by the wise, Venerable Sir.)

"If these things are acted upon, will they bring about harm and suffering, or not. What do you think?"

(Answer: When put into practice, these things bring about harm and suffering, this is our view on this matter.)

"In that case, *Kālāmas*, when I said, 'Come, *Kālāmas*, do not believe simply because a belief has been adhered to for generations ... nor simply because this man is your teacher, or is revered by you. But when you know for yourselves that these things are unskilful, then you should abandon those things', it is on account of this that I thus spoke."[18]

The following passage is from an exchange between King Pasenadi of Kosala and the Venerable *Ānanda*. It is a series of questions and answers relating to the nature of good and evil, from which it can be seen that Venerable *Ānanda* makes use of all the standards mentioned above.

King: Venerable Sir, when foolish, unintelligent people, not carefully considering, speak in praise or blame of others, I do not take their words seriously. As for pundits, the wise and astute, who carefully consider before praising or criticizing, I give weight to their words.

Venerable *Ānanda*, which kinds of bodily actions, verbal actions and mental actions would, on reflection, be censured by wise ascetics and Brahmins?

Ānanda: They are those actions of body ... speech ... mind that are unskilful, Your Majesty.

King: What are those actions of body ... speech ... mind that are unskilful?

Ānanda: They are those actions of body ... speech ... mind that are harmful.

King: What are those actions of body ... speech ... mind that are harmful?

Ānanda: They are those actions of body ... speech ... mind that are oppressive.

King: What are those actions of body ... speech ... mind that are oppressive?

Ānanda: They are those actions of body ... speech ... mind which result in suffering.

King: What are those actions of body ... speech ... mind which result in suffering?

Ānanda: Those actions of body ... speech ... mind which serve to torment oneself, to torment others, or to torment both; which bring about an increase in unskilful conditions and a decrease of skilful conditions; Your Majesty, just these kinds of actions of body ... speech ... mind are censured by wise ascetics and Brahmins.

Following that, Venerable *Ānanda* answered the king's

questions about skilful conditions in the same way, summarizing with:

"Those actions of body ... speech ... mind which result in happiness, that is, those actions which do not serve to torment oneself, to torment others, nor to torment both; which bring about a decrease in unskilful conditions and an increase in skilful conditions; Your Majesty, just these kinds of actions of body ... speech ... mind are not censured by wise ascetics and Brahmins."[19]

"One in the power of greed and desire ... hatred and resentment ... delusion ... with mind thus distorted ... does not know as it is what is useful to oneself ... what is useful to others ... what is useful to both sides. Having abandoned desire ... aversion ... delusion, one knows clearly what is useful to oneself ... useful to others ... useful to both."[20]

"Bad *kamma* is like freshly squeezed milk ... it takes time to sour. Bad *kamma* follows and burns the evil doer just like hot coals buried in ash."[21]

"One who previously made bad *kamma*, but who reforms and creates good *kamma*, brightens the world like the moon appearing from behind a cloud."[22]

"To make good *kamma* is like having a good friend at your side."[23]

"*Ānanda!* For those bad actions through body, speech and mind, which are discouraged by me, the following consequences can be expected: one is blame-worthy to oneself; the wise, on careful consideration, find one censurable; a bad reputation spreads; one dies confused; and at death, on the breaking up of the body, one goes to the woeful states, the nether realms, hell ...

"*Ānanda!* For those good actions through body, speech and mind recommended by me, the following rewards can be expected: one is not blameworthy to oneself; the wise, after careful consideration, find one praiseworthy; a good reputation spreads; one dies unconfused; and at death, on the breaking up of the body, one attains to a pleasant realm, to heaven ..."[24]

"*Bhikkhus*, abandon unskilful conditions. Unskilful conditions can be abandoned. If it were impossible to abandon unskilful conditions, I would not tell you to do so ... but because unskilful conditions can be abandoned, thus do I tell you ... Moreover, if the abandoning of those unskilful conditions was not conducive to welfare, but to suffering, I would not say, '*Bhikkhus*, abandon unskilful conditions', but because the abandoning of these unskilful conditions is conducive to benefit and happiness, so I say, '*Bhikkhus*, abandon unskilful conditions.'

"*Bhikkhus*, cultivate skilful conditions. Skilful conditions can be cultivated. If it were impossible to cultivate skilful conditions, I would not tell you to do so ... but because skilful conditions can be cultivated, thus do I tell you ... Moreover, if the cultivation of those skilful conditions was not conducive to welfare, but to suffering, I would not tell you to cultivate skilful conditions, but because the cultivation of skilful conditions is conducive to welfare and to happiness, thus do I say, '*Bhikkhus*, cultivate skilful conditions.'"[25]

"*Bhikkhus*, there are those things which should be abandoned with the body, not the speech; there are those things which should be abandoned with the speech, not the body; there are those things which should be abandoned neither with the body, nor speech, but must be clearly seen with wisdom (in the mind) and then abandoned.

"What are those things which should be abandoned with the body, not through speech? Herein, a *bhikkhu* in this Dhamma-Vinaya*, incurs transgressions through the body. His wise companions in the Dhamma, having considered the matter, say to him: 'Venerable friend, you have incurred these offences. It would be well if you were to abandon this wrong

---

* Dhamma-Vinaya: literally, 'Teaching and Discipline: a name used by the Buddha to refer to his Teaching.

bodily behaviour and cultivate good bodily behaviour.' Having been so instructed by those wise companions, he abandons those wrong bodily actions and cultivates good ones. This is a condition which should be abandoned by body, not by speech.

"What are the things which should be abandoned through speech, not through the body? Herein, a *bhikkhu* in this Dhamma-Vinaya incurs some transgressions through speech. His wise companions in the Dhamma, having considered the matter, say to him: 'Venerable Friend, you have incurred these offences of speech. It would be well if you were to relinquish this wrong speech and cultivate good speech.' Having been so instructed by those wise companions, he abandons that wrong speech and cultivates good speech. This is a condition which should be abandoned by speech, not by body.

"What are the things which should be abandoned neither by body or speech, but which should be clearly understood with wisdom and then abandoned? They are greed ... hatred ... delusion ... anger ... vindictiveness ... spite ... arrogance ... meanness. These things should be abandoned neither by the body or speech, but should be clearly understood with wisdom and then abandoned." [26]

3 THE FRUITION OF KAMMA

Results of *kamma* on different levels

PROBABLY the most misunderstood aspect of the whole subject of *kamma* is the way it yields results, with doubts centring around the principle, 'Good actions bring good results, bad actions bring bad results.' Is this really true? To some, it seems that in 'the real world' there are many who have obtained good results from bad actions, and bad results from good actions. This kind of understanding arises from confusion between 'Social Convention' and the law of *kamma*. This can be readily seen from the way people confuse even the meaning of the words, 'good actions bring good results'. Instead of understanding the meaning as 'in performing good actions, there is goodness', or 'good actions bring about good results in accordance with the law of *kamma*', they take the meaning to be 'good actions result in good things'. With this in mind, we should now consider the matter in more depth.

The subject which causes doubt is the distinction, and the relationship between, the law of *kamma* and Social Convention. To clarify this point, let us first consider the fruition of *kamma* on four different levels:

1. The inner, mental level: the results *kamma* has within the mind itself, in the form of accumulated tendencies, both skilful and unskilful, and the quality of the mind … its happiness, suffering, and so on.

2. The physical level: the effect *kamma* has on character, mannerisms, bearing, behavioural tendencies. The results on this level are derived from the first level, and their fields of relevance overlap, but here we are considering them separately in order to further clarify the way these two levels affect life experiences.

3. The level of life experiences: how *kamma* affects the events of life, producing both desirable and undesirable experiences; specifically, such external events as prosperity and decline; failure and success; wealth, status, happiness and praise, and the many forms of loss which are their opposites. Together these are known as the *lokadhamma* (worldly conditions). The results of *kamma* on this level can be further divided into two branches:

– those arising from external causes in the environment, other than people.

– those from causes related to other people and society.

4. The social level: the results of individual and collective *kamma* on society, leading to social prosperity or decline, harmony or discord. This also includes the effects resulting from man's interaction with his environment.

It can be observed that levels 1 and 2 refer to the results which affect mind and character, which are the fields in which the law of *kamma* is dominant. The third level is where the law of *kamma* and Social Convention meet, and it is at this point that confusion arises. This is the problem which we will now consider. The fourth level, *kamma* on the social level, will be considered in the next Chapter.

When considering the meaning of the words 'good actions bring good results, bad actions bring bad results', most people tend to take note only of the results given on the third level, those from external sources, completely ignoring results on levels one and two. However, these first two levels are of prime importance, not only in themselves, determining mental well-being, inner strength or shortcomings, and the maturity or weakness of the faculties, but also in determining external events. That is to say, that portion of results on the third level which comes into the domain of *kammaniyāma* extends from the kamma-results on the first and second levels.

For instance, states of mind which are results of *kamma* on the first level – interests, preferences, tendencies, methods for finding happiness or coping with suffering – will influence not only the way we look at things, but also the situations we are drawn to, reactions or decisions made, our way of life and the experiences or results encountered. They also affect the attitude we adopt towards life's experiences, which will in turn affect the second level (behavioural tendencies). This in turn promotes the way in which mental activities (the first level) affect external events (the third level). The direction, style, or method taken for action, the persistence with it, the particular obstacles in face of which we will yield and in face of which we will persist, including the probability of success, are all influenced by character and attitude.

This is not to deny that other factors, particularly environmental and social ones, affect each other and have an influence over the individual, but here we are concerned more with observing how the workings of *kamma* on the internal level effect results on the external level.

Although the effects of *kamma* on the third level, the events of life and the results thereof, are largely derived from the effects of the *kammaniyāma* from the personal (physical and mental) level, this is not always the case. For example, an honest and capable public servant who applied himself to his work would seem likely to advance in his career, at least more so than one who was inefficient and inept. But sometimes the results don't work out that way. This is because events in life are not entirely subject to the *kammaniyāma*. There are factors involved from other *niyāma* and value-systems, especially Social Convention. If there were only *kammaniyāma* there would be no problem, results would arise in direct correspondence with the relevant *kamma*. But looking only at the influence of *kammaniyāma* to the exclusion of other factors, and failing to distinguish between the natural laws and Social Conventions involved, causes confusion, and this is precisely what causes the belief, 'good actions bring bad results; bad actions bring good results'.

For example, a conscientious student who applies himself to his lessons should acquire learning. But there may be times when he is physically exhausted or has a headache. The weather may be extremely hot, in which case he may not finish the book he is reading, or may not take it all in, or some accident may interrupt his reading. Whatever the case, we can still assert that in general, *kammaniyāma* is the prime determining factor for the good and bad experiences of life.

Let us now look at and rectify some of the misunderstandings in regard to the fruition of *kamma* by referring to the root texts. The phrase that Thai people like to repeat, "good actions bring good results, bad actions bring bad results", comes from the Buddha's statement,

**Yādisaṁ vapate bījaṁ   Tādisaṁ labhate phalaṁ
Kalayāṇakārī kalayāṇaṁ   Pāpakārī ca pāpakaṁ**

Which translates as:
**As the seed, so the fruit.
Who does good, receives good,
Who does bad, receives bad.**[27]

This passage most clearly and succinctly expresses the Buddhist doctrine of *kamma*. Note that here the Buddha uses *bījaniyāma* (the law of heredity) for a comparison. Simply by clearly considering this simile, we can allay all confusion regarding the law of *kamma* and Social Convention. That is to say, the phrase, 'As the seed, so the fruit', explains the natural law pertaining to plants: if tamarind is planted, you get tamarind; if grapes are planted, you get grapes; if lettuce is planted, you get lettuce. It does not speak at all in terms of Social Convention, such as in 'if tamarind is planted, you get money', or 'planting lettuce will make you rich', which are different stages of the process. *Bījaniyāma* and Social Convention become related when, having planted grapes, for example, and obtained grapes, and the time being coincident with a good price for grapes, then your grapes are sold for a good price, and you get rich that year. But at another time, you may plant water melons, and reap a good harvest, but that year everybody plants water melons, supply

41

exceeds demand, and the price of water melons goes down. You make a loss and have to throw away a lot of water melons. Apart from the factor of market demand, there may also be other factors involved, economic factors determined by Social Convention. But the essential point is the certainty of the natural law of heredity, and the distinction between that natural law and Social Convention. They are different and yet clearly related.

People tend to look at the law of *kamma* and Social Convention as one and the same thing, interpreting 'good actions bring good results' as meaning 'good actions will make us rich', or 'good actions will earn a promotion', which in some cases seems quite reasonable. But things do not always go that way. To say this is just like saying, "Plant mangoes and you'll get a lot of money", or "They planted apples, that's why they're hard up". These things may be true, or may not be. But what can be said is that this kind of thinking jumps ahead of the facts a step or two. It is not entirely true. It may be sufficient to communicate on an everyday basis, but if you really want to speak the truth, you must analyse the pertinent factors more clearly.

Factors which affect the fruition of *kamma*

In the Pali there are four pairs of factors which influence the fruition of *kamma* on the level of life experiences. They are given as the four advantages (*sampatti*) and the four disadvantages (*vipatti*).[28]

Sampatti translates roughly as 'attribute', and refers to the confluence of factors to support the fruition of good *kamma* and obstruct the fruition of bad *kamma*. The four are:

1. **Gatisampatti:** Favourable birthplace, favourable environment, circumstances or career; that is, to be born into a favourable area, locality or country; and on a short term scale, to live in or go to a favourable place.

2. **Upadhisampatti:** The asset, suitability and support of

the body; that is, to have a beautiful or pleasant appearance or personality which arouses respect or favour; a strong and healthy body, etc.

3. *Kālasampatti:* The asset of opportunity, aptness of time, or the support of time; that is, to be born at a time when the country lives in peace and harmony, the government is good, people live virtuously, praise goodness and do not support corruption; on an immediate level, to encounter opportunities at the right time, at the right moment.

4. *Payogasampatti:* The attribute of action, aptness of action, or advantage of action; that is, action which is appropriate to the circumstance; action which is in concordance with personal skill or capability; action which fully accords with the principles or criteria concerned; thorough-going, not half-hearted, action; relevant procedure or method.

Vipatti translates roughly as 'defect' or 'weakness', and refers to a tendency within conditioning factors to encourage the fruition of bad *kamma* rather than the good. They are:

1. *Gativipatti:* Unfavourable birthplace, unfavourable environment, circumstances or career; that is, to be born into a sphere, locality, country or environment which is regressive, ill-suited, unsupportive.

2. *Upadhivipatti:* Weakness or defectiveness of the body; that is, to have a deformed or sickly body, of unpleasant appearance, having ungainly mannerisms and personality. This includes times of bad health and illness.

3. *Kālavipatti:* Disadvantage or defectiveness of time; that is, to be born into an age when there is social unrest, bad government, a degenerate society, oppression of good people, praise of the bad, and so on. This also includes inopportune action.

4 *Payogavipatti:* Weakness or defectiveness of action; putting effort into a task or matter which is worthless, or for which one is not capable; action which is not thoroughly carried through.

First pair: *Gatisampatti:* Birth into an affluent community and a good education can procure a higher position in society than for another who, although brighter and more diligent, is born into a poorer community with less opportunity. *Gativipatti:* At a time when a Buddha is born into the world and expounding the Dhamma, birth in a primitive jungle or as a hell-being will obstruct any chance of hearing the teachings; learning and capability in a community where such talents are not appreciated may lead to rejection and scorn.

    Second pair: *Upadhisampatti:* Attractive features and a pleasant appearance can often be utilized to shift upwards on the social scale and procure success. *Upadhivipatti:* Deformity or deficiency are likely to hinder the honour and prestige that would normally befall a member of a socially high and wealthy family; where two people have otherwise equal attributes, but one is attractive while the other is unpleasant looking or sickly, the attributes of the body may be the deciding factor for success.

    Third pair; *Kālasampatti:* At a time when government and society are honest and praise goodness, honesty and rectitude can procure advancement; at a time when poetry is socially preferred, a poet is likely to become famous and revered. *Kālavipatti:* At a time when society has fallen from righteousness and the government is corrupt, honest people may actually be persecuted; at a time when a large portion of society prefers harsh music, a musician skilled at cool and relaxing music may receive little recognition.

    Fourth pair: *Payogasampatti:* Even without goodness or talent, a knack with public relations and an understanding of social mores can help to override failings in other areas; a skill in forging documents, for example, could be beneficially turned to the inspection of references. *Payogavipatti:* Talent and abilities will inevitably be impaired by an addiction to gambling; a sprinter with the ability to become a champion athlete might misuse his talent for running away with other people's goods; a practically minded man with a mechanical bent might go to work in a clerical position for which he is wholly unsuited.

The fruits of *kamma* on the external level are mostly worldly conditions, which are in a state of constant flux. These worldly conditions are relatively superficial, they are not the real essence of life. Whether they have a heavy or light influence depends on the extent of attachment to them. If there is no attachment it is possible to maintain equilibrium and live content in the face of hardships, or at least not be overwhelmed by them. For this reason Buddhism encourages intelligent reflection and understanding of the truth of this world, to have mindfulness and not be heedless: at pleasant times, times of gain, not to become intoxicated, and at unpleasant times, times of loss, not to fall into depression or anxiety, but to carefully consider problems with wisdom.

Aspiration to worldly goals should be coupled with a knowledge of personal attributes and weaknesses, and the ability to choose and organize the relevant attributes to attain those goals through skilful means *(kusala kamma)*. Such actions will have a lasting and beneficial effect on life at all levels. Success sought through unskilful means, or favourable occasions used to create unskilful *kamma*, will create undesirable results according to the *kammaniyāma*. These four advantages *(sampatti)* and disadvantages *(vipatti)* are in a state of constant change. When favourable times or opportunities have passed, evil *kamma* will ripen. Favourable conditions should rather be utilized to create good *kamma*.

In this context, we might summarize by saying that, for any given action, where many different natural laws come into play, our prime emphasis should be with the factors of *kamma*. This should be our firm resolve and basis for action above all else. As for the factors which come under other kinds of natural law, after careful consideration, they can also be incorporated, as long as they are not harmful on the level of *kamma*. Practising in this way can be called 'utilizing skilful *kamma* and the four advantages', or 'knowing how to benefit from both the law of *kamma* and Social Conventions'.

In any case, bearing in mind the real aim of the Buddha's teaching, an aspiration to true goodness should not be traded for merely worldly results (wealth, position, praise and happiness). **Truly good kamma arises from one or another of the three roots of skilfulness, *non-greed, non-aversion* and *non-delusion*.** These are actions based on altruism, relinquishing the unskilful within the mind and developing benevolent thoughts towards others, creating actions based on goodwill and compassion. These are actions based on wisdom, a mind which aspires to truth and enlightenment. This can be regarded as the highest kind of *kamma,* the *kamma* which leads to the cessation of *kamma.*

Understanding the process of fruition

Whenever the intention to perform skilful or unskilful deeds arises, that is the beginning of movement in the mind. To use a more scientific phrase, we could say that 'volition-energy' has arisen. How this energy proceeds, which determinants affect it and so on, are usually a mystery to people, in which they take little interest. They tend to devote more interest to the results which appear clearly at the end of the cycle, especially those which materialize in the human social sphere. These are things which are easily seen and spoken about.

Mankind has a very good knowledge of the creations of the mind on a material plane, and how these things come about, but about the actual nature of the mind itself, the seat of intention, and the way intention affects life and the psyche, we have very little knowledge indeed. We could even say that this is a dark and mysterious area for most people. This in spite of the fact that we must have an intimate relationship with these things and are directly influenced by them.

On account of this obscurity and ignorance, when confronted with seemingly random or unexplainable events, people tend to be unable to join the scattered threads of cause and effect, and either fail to see all the relevant determining factors, or see them incompletely. They then proceed to blame other things, rejecting the law of *kamma.* This is tantamount to rejecting the law of cause and effect, or the natural process of inter-dependence. Rejecting the law of *kamma* and blaming various other factors for the misfortunes in life is in itself productive of more unskilful *kamma*. Namely, by so doing, any chance of improving unfavourable situations through clear understanding is frustrated.

In any case, it is recognized that the process of *kamma* fruition is extremely intricate, one that is beyond the ability of most people to fathom. In the Pali it is said to be *acinteyya,* that is, beyond the comprehension of the normal thought processes. The Buddha said that to insist on thinking about such things could drive you crazy. In saying this, the Buddha was not so much forbidding any consideration of the law of *kamma*, but rather pointing out that the intricacy of causes and events in nature cannot be understood through thought alone, but only through direct knowledge.

Thus, being *acinteyya* does not forbid us from touching the subject at all. Our relationship with *kamma* is one of knowledge and a firm conviction in that knowledge, based on examination of those things which we are able to know. These are the things which are actually manifesting in the present moment, beginning with the most immediate and extending outwards. On the immediate level we are dealing with the thought process, or intention, as has been described above, initially noticing how skilful thoughts benefit the psyche and unskilful thoughts harm it. From there the fruits of these thoughts spread outwards to affect others and the world at large, rebounding to affect the doer in correspondingly beneficial and harmful ways.

We can observe this process of fruition on increasingly intricate levels, influenced by innumerable external causes, until we are able to see a complexity far exceeding anything previously conceived of. Such an awareness will provide a firm conviction in the truth of the natural law of cause and effect. Once the process is understood on an immediate level, the long term basis is also understood, because the long term is derived from the immediate present. Without an understanding of the process on the short term, it is impossible to understand the process on a long term basis. Only in this way can we understand things in accordance with the Dhamma.

Having a firm conviction in the natural process of cause and effect in relation to intention or volition is to have a firm conviction in the law of *kamma,* or to believe in *kamma.* With a firm conviction in the law of *kamma,* aspirations can be realized through appropriate action, with a clear understanding of the cause and effect involved. When any goal is desired, both in the area of personal welfare *(kammaniyāma)* and in the area of worldly conditions, the relevant factors, included in both the law of *kamma* and in other *niyāma,* should be carefully considered and then the right conditions created.

For example, a clever artist or craftsman will not only consider his own designs and intentions to the exclusion of everything else, but also the relevant factors from other *niyāma* and value-systems. When applying an intricate house design from his mind into a material object, an architect must consider the materials to be used for particular areas. If he designates a softwood for use where a hardwood is needed, no matter how beautiful the design of that house may be, it may collapse without fulfilling the function it was intended for.

At this stage it should be stressed that to work with the law of *kamma* in a skilful way, it is necessary to develop *kusalachanda* or *dhammachanda*,* to encourage an interest in the Dhamma, an appreciation of goodness, and an aspiration to improve life and the environment. A desire for quality or care in personal actions and relationships is necessary. If the desire is for only worldly results, lacking this *kusala-* or *Dhamma-chanda,* the tendency is to attempt to play with or cheat the law of *kamma,* causing trouble not only on the individual level, but for society and mankind as a whole.

---

* *Kusalachanda*: desire to act skilfully, or to create wholesome conditions; *Dhammachanda*: desire for what is good, or what is in accord with the Dhamma. For a more detailed description of 'chanda', see Chapter 5.

Fruits of *Kamma* on a long term basis – Heaven and Hell

Some scholars feel that in order to convince the layman of the law of *kamma* and to induce him to lead a moral life, he must first be convinced of the fruition of *kamma* on the long term, from past lives and into future lives. As a result of this, it is considered necessary to verify the existence of an afterlife, or at least to present some convincing evidence to support it. Some have attempted to explain the principle of *kamma* and afterlife by referring to modern scientific laws, such as The Law of Conservation of Energy, applying it to the workings of the mind and intention. Others refer to the theories of modern psychology, investigating data concerning recollection of past lives. Some even go so far as to use mediums and seances to support their claims. These attempts at scientific verification will not be enumerated here because they are beyond the scope of this book. Those interested are advised to look into the matter for themselves from any of the numerous books available on the subject. As far as the present book goes, only a few reflections on the matter will be given.

The necessity of demonstrating the truth of future lives and the fruits of *kamma* on a long term basis before there can be acceptance of an ethical teaching would seem to contain some measure of validity. If people really did believe these things, it is possible that they would be more inclined to shun bad actions and cultivate good ones. Those who have this view can therefore be said to be speaking with some justification and with good intention. It would thus seem unnecessary to oppose their continued study and experimentation, as long as it lies within the bounds of reason. (Otherwise, such investigations, instead of casting light on the mysterious, may turn observable truths into inexplicable mysteries!) If there is honest and reasoned experimentation, at the very least some scientific gain is to be expected.

On the other hand, scholars who are delving into such

matters should not become so immersed in their research that they are blinded by it, seeing its importance above all else and overlooking the importance of the present moment. This becomes an extreme or unbalanced view. Too much stress on rebirth into heaven and hell realms results in neglect of the good which should be aspired to in the present.

In addition to this, our original intention to encourage moral conscience at all times, including future lives, and an unshakable faith in the law of *kamma,* will result instead in an aspiration only for future results, which becomes a kind of greed. Good actions are performed for the sake of profit. Over-emphasis on future lives ignores the importance of *kusalachanda* and *dhammachanda,* which in turn becomes a denial of, or even an insult to, the human ability to practise and develop truth and righteousness for their own sakes.

Even though there is some validity to the idea that verification of an afterlife might influence people to lead more virtuous lives, still there is no reason why we should have to wait to be satisfied on this point before we will agree to do so. It is impossible to tell when the big 'if' of this scientific research will be answered: when will this research be completed? And if we consider the matter strictly according to the meaning of the word 'verification', as being a clear demonstration, then the word is invalid in this instance. It is impossible for one person to resolve another's doubts about rebirth. Rebirth is something which only those who see for themselves can really be sure about. This 'verification' that is spoken of is merely an assemblage of related facts and case histories for analysis or speculation. The real essence of the matter remains *acinteyya,* unfathomable. No matter how many facts people amass to support the issue, for most it will remain a matter of faith or belief. As long as it is still a matter of belief, there will always be those who disbelieve, and there will always be the possibility of doubt within those who

believe. Only when certain of the fetters* have been abandoned on the attainment of Stream Entry** is it possible to
be beyond doubt.

To sum up, searching for data and personal histories to support the issue of life after death has some benefit, and such doings
should not be discouraged. But to say that the practice of Dhamma
must depend on the verification of these things is neither true nor
desirable.

Summary: Verifying Future Lives

'Are there really past and future lives, heaven and hell?' This
question not only fascinates people, but also disquiets them, because
it is an unknown quantity. Therefore I would like to include a small
summary of the matter.

1.   According to the teachings of Buddhism as preserved in the
     scriptures, these things do exist.
2.   There is no conclusion to verifying them because they cannot
     be proven one way or another. You either believe in them or
     you don't. Neither those who believe nor those who disbe-
     lieve, nor those who are trying to prove or disprove, really
     know where life comes from or where it goes to, either their
     own or others'. All are in darkness, not only about the distant
     past, but even toward their present birth, their present lives,
     and the future, even one day away.
3.   On the subject of verification: it can be said that 'sights must
     be seen with the eye, sounds must be heard with the ear,
     flavours must be tasted with the tongue' and so on. It would

---

* The ten fetters, or *Saṁyojana,* are the bonds which bind human consciousness to the samsaric world. They are: Self view, doubt, blind
attachment to rites and practices, sensual desire, aversion, desire for form
(concentration states), desire for formless (concentration states), restlessness, conceit and ignorance.
** *Sotāpanna,* or Stream Enterer: one who has transcended the first three
fetters mentioned above through transcendent insight.

be impossible to see a visual object using organs other than the eye, even if you used ten ears and ten tongues to do so. Similarly, perceiving visual or audible objects (such as ultraviolet light waves or supersonic sound waves) with instruments of disparate or incompatible wave length is impossible. Some things are visible to a cat, but even ten human eyes cannot see them. Some things, although audible to a bat, are inaudible to even ten human ears. In this context, death and birth are experiences of life, or to be more precise, events of the mind, and must be researched by life or the mind. Any research should therefore be carried out in one of the following ways:

a) In order to verify the truth of these things in the mind, it is said that the mind must first be in the state of concentrated calm, or *samādhi*. However, if this method seems impractical or inconvenient, or is considered to be prone to self-deception, then the next method is

b) to verify with this present life itself. None of us have ever died. The only thorough test is that achieved with one's own death.... but few seem inclined to try this method.

c) If there is no real testing as mentioned above, all that remains is to show a number of case histories and collected data, such as accounts of recollections of previous lives, or to use comparisons from other fields, such as sounds perceptible only to certain instruments, and so on, to show that these things do have some credibility. However, the issue remains on the level of belief.

Regardless of belief or disbelief, or however people try to prove these things to one another, the unavoidable fact, from which all future life must stem, is life in the present moment. Given this, it follows that this is where we should be directing our attention. In Buddhism, which is considered to be a practical religion, the real point of interest is our practical relationship towards this present life. How are we going to conduct our lives as they unfold right now?

How are we going to make our present life a good one, and at the same time, in the event that there is a future life, ensure that it will be good? In the light of these points, we might consider the following:

– In the original Pali, that is in the discourses (Suttas), there is very little mention of previous and future lives, heaven and hell. In most cases they are merely given a mention. This indicates that not much importance or relevance is attributed to them in comparison to the conduct of life in the present world, or the practices of *sīla, samādhi* and *paññā**.

– When, in the Pali, rebirth in heaven or hell is included in the fruits of good and evil *kamma,* it is usually after mentioning all the fruits of *kamma* occurring in the present life. These may be given as four, five or up to ten in number, with the final phrase: "At death, on the breaking up of the body, he goes to the nether worlds, a woeful state, hell", or "At death, on the breaking up of the body, he goes to a pleasant bourn, heaven."

There are two observations to be made here:

Firstly, the fruits of *kamma* in the present life are given priority and are described in detail. Results in an afterlife seem to be thrown in at the end to 'round off the discussion', so to speak.

Secondly, the Buddha's explanation of the good and bad results of *kamma* was always as a demonstration of the truth that these things proceed according to causes. That is, the results (of *kamma)* follow automatically from their causes. Simply to know this fact is to give confidence in the fruits of actions.

As long as those who do not believe in an afterlife still do not know for a fact that there is no afterlife, or heaven and hell, they will be unable to completely refute the doubts lurking deeply within

---

* Moral discipline, mental discipline, or concentration, and wisdom.

their minds. When such people have spent the energy of their youth and old age is advancing, they tend to experience fear of the future, which, if they have not led a virtuous life, becomes very distressing. Therefore, to be completely certain, even those who do not believe in these things should develop goodness. Whether there is or is not an afterlife, they can be at peace.

As for those who believe, they should ensure that their belief is based on an understanding of the truth of cause and effect. That is, they should see results in a future life as ensuing from the quality of the mind developed in the present life, giving emphasis to the creation of good *kamma* in the present. This kind of emphasis will ensure that any relationship with a future life will be one of confidence, based on the present moment. Aspirations for a future life will thus encourage care with the conduct of the present moment, bearing in mind the principle: "Regardless of how you relate to the next life, do not give it more importance than the present one." This way, the mistake of performing good deeds as a kind of investment made for profit is avoided.

Any belief in a future life should help to alleviate or discard altogether dependence on higher powers or things occult. This is because belief in a future life means belief in the efficacy of one's own actions *(kamma)*. If one is to progress along the wheel of Samsāra*, dependence on any external power will only serve to weaken and slow one down within it. Those who have allowed themselves to slide into such dependencies should strive to extract themselves from them and become more self-reliant.

Ideally, we should try to advance to the stage of avoiding bad actions and developing the good regardless of belief or disbelief. This means to perform good deeds without the need for a result in some future life, and to avoid evil actions even if you don't believe in a future life. This can be achieved by:

---

* The Wheel of Birth and Death – to 'progress along the Wheel of Birth and Death' means to attain to progressively higher and more favourable births through the practice of good actions.

1) developing *kusalachanda* or *Dhammachanda* to such a level that there arises a predilection for the true and the good, an aspiration for goodness and rectitude, and a desire for the best in all situations.

2) developing an appreciation for the subtle happiness of inner peace, and making that in itself an instrument for preventing the arising of evil states of mind and for encouraging the good. This is because it is necessary to avoid bad actions and cultivate the good in order to experience this inner peace. In addition, inner peace is an important aid in resisting the attraction of sensual desire, thus preventing the creation of the more extreme forms of bad *kamma*. However, concerning the state of inner peace, as long as it is on the worldly level*, it is advisable to be wary of getting so caught up in it as to cease to progress in the Dhamma (by allowing it to become an object of attachment, causing stagnation and thus preventing further development).

3) training the mind to conduct life with wisdom, knowing the truth of the world and life, or knowing the truth of conditions *(sankhāra)*. This enables the mind to have some degree of freedom from material things or sense pleasures, thus reducing the likelihood of committing bad *kamma* on their account. A sensitivity to the lives and feelings of others is developed, understanding their pleasures, pains and desires, so that there is more a desire to help rather than to take advantage of. This can be regarded as the life style of one who has reached, or is practising towards, the transcendent *(lokuttara)* Dhamma and transcendent Right View**. Failing this, to live by the faith which is the forerunner of that

---

* *Samādhi,* or concentration, is sometimes divided into two levels. On the worldly level are the Four levels of *jhāna,* absorption, in the mind of the worldling, one who has still not experienced transcendent insight. On the transcendent level, *samādhi* is those same four *jhānas,* but occurring in the mind of one who has experienced transcendent insight.
** *Lokuttara sammā-diṭṭhi*

wisdom. This is the faith which is an unshakable conviction in a life guided by liberating wisdom as the finest and most excellent kind of life. From there follows the effort to live up to the ideal of such a life.

Actually these three principles of practice are connected and support each other. In particular, point number 1) *(chanda)* is necessary in performing any kind of good action, so is also essential in points 2) concentration *(samādhi)* and 3) wisdom, *(paññā)*.

When accompanied by practice in accordance with these three principles, any belief in fruition of *kamma* in a future life will serve to encourage and strengthen the avoidance of bad actions and development of the good. Such belief will not in itself be so critical that without expectation of good results in a future life there will no longer be any incentive to do good deeds.

If it is not possible to practise these three principles, then belief in a future life can be used to encourage a more moral life, which is better than letting people live their lives obsessed with the search for sensual gratification, which only serves to increase exploitation on both the individual and social levels. In addition, belief in a future life is considered to be mundane Right View* and thus is one step on the way to developing a good life.

Kamma fruition according to the *Cūla Kammavibhaṅga Sutta*

Having established an initial understanding, let us now look at one of the Buddha's classic teachings dealing with the fruition of *kamma*, extending from the present into a future life.

"See here, young man. Beings are the owners of their *kamma*, heirs to their *kamma*, born of their *kamma*, have *kamma* as their lineage, have *kamma* as their support. *Kamma* it is which distinguishes beings into fine and coarse states."

---

* *Lokiya sammā-diṭṭhi*

56

1.a. A woman or a man is given to killing living beings, is ruthless, kills living beings constantly and is lacking in goodwill or compassion. At death, on account of that *kamma*, developed and nurtured within, that person goes to a woeful bourn, the nether worlds, to hell. Or if not reborn in hell, but in the human world, he or she will be short-lived.

b. A woman or man shuns killing and is possessed of goodwill and compassion. At death, on account of that *kamma*, developed and nurtured within, that person goes to a good bourn, to a heaven realm. Or, if not reborn in heaven, but as a human being, he or she will be blessed with longevity.

2.a A woman or man is given to harming other beings by the hand and the weapon. At death, on account of that *kamma*, developed and nurtured within, that person goes to a woeful bourn, the nether worlds, to hell. Or, if not reborn in hell, but as a human being, he or she will be sickly.

b. A woman or man shuns harming other beings. At death, on account of that *kamma*, developed and nurtured within, that person arrives at a good bourn, a heaven realm. Or, if not reborn in heaven, but as a human being, he or she will be one with few illnesses.

3.a. A woman or man is of ill temper, is quick to hatred, offended at the slightest criticism, harbours hatred and displays anger. At death, on account of that *kamma*, developed and nurtured within, that person goes to a woeful bourn, the nether worlds, to hell. Or, if not born in hell, but as a human being, he or she will be ugly.

b. A woman or a man is not easily angered. At death, on account of that *kamma*, developed and nurtured within, that person goes to a pleasant bourn, a heaven realm. Or, if not reborn in heaven, but as a human being, he or she will be of pleasant appearance.

4.a. A woman or man has a jealous mind. When others receive awards, honour and respect, he or she is ill at ease and angry. At death, on account of that *kamma,* developed and nurtured within, that person goes to a woeful bourn, the nether worlds, to hell. Or, if not reborn in hell, but as a human being, he or she will be one of little influence.

b. A woman or a man is one who harbours no jealousy. At death, on account of that *kamma,* developed and nurtured within, that person goes to a good bourn, to a heaven realm. Or, if not reborn in heaven, but as a human being, he or she will be powerful and influential.

5.a. A woman or man is not one who gives, does not share out food, water and clothing. At death, on account of that *kamma,* developed and nurtured within, that person goes to a woeful bourn, the nether worlds, to hell. Or, if not reborn in hell, but as a human being, he or she will be poor.

b. A woman or a man is one who practises giving, who shares out food, water and clothing. At death, on account of that *kamma,* developed and nurtured within, that person goes to a good bourn, to a heaven realm. Or, if not reborn in heaven, but as a human being, he or she will be wealthy.

6.a. A woman or man is stubborn and unyielding, proud, arrogant and disrespectful to those who should be respected. At death, on account of that *kamma,* developed and nurtured within, that person goes to a woeful bourn, the nether worlds, to hell. Or, if not reborn in hell, but as a human being, he or she will be born into a low family.

b. A woman or man is not stubborn or unyielding, not proud, but pays respect and takes an interest in those who should be respected. At death, on account of that *kamma,* developed and nurtured within, that person goes to a good bourn, to a heaven realm. Or, if not reborn in heaven, but as a human being, he or she will be born into a high family.

7.a. A woman or man neither visits nor questions ascetics and Brahmins about what is good, what is evil, what is harmful, what is not harmful, what should be done and what should not be done; which actions lead to suffering, which actions will lead to lasting happiness. At death, on account of that *kamma*, developed and nurtured within, that person goes to a woeful bourn, the nether worlds, to hell. Or, if not reborn in hell, but as a human being, he or she will be of little intelligence.

b. A woman or man seeks out and questions ascetics and Brahmins about what is good and so on. At death, on account of that *kamma*, developed and nurtured within, that person goes to a good bourn, to a heaven realm. Or, if not reborn in heaven, but as a human being, he or she will be intelligent. [29]

In this *Sutta*, although fruition in a future life is spoken of, yet it is the actions of the present moment, particularly those which have become regular, which are emphasized. Regular actions are the factors which form the qualities of the mind and help to form personality and character. These are the forces which bring about results in direct relation to the causes. Rewards of such actions are not fantastic, such as in doing one single good deed, an act of giving, for example, and receiving some boundless reward fulfilling all wishes and desires. If this sort of attitude prevails it only causes people to do good deeds as an investment, like saving money in a bank and sitting around waiting for the interest to grow; or like people who play the lottery, putting down a tiny investment and expecting a huge reward. As a result they pay no attention to their daily behaviour and take no interest in conducting a good life as is explained in this *Sutta*.

Summarizing, the essence of the *Cūla Kammavibhaṅga Sutta* still rests on the fact that any deliberation about results in a future life should be based on a firm conviction in the *kamma*, that is, the quality of the mind and of conduct, which is being made in the present moment. The results of actions on a long term basis are derived from and related to these causes.

A basic principle in this regard might be summarized as follows: The correct attitude to results of *kamma* in future lives must be one which promotes and strengthens *Dhammachanda* (desire for goodness). Any belief in *kamma*-results which does not strengthen *Dhammachanda*, but instead serves to strengthen greed and desire, should be recognized as a mistaken kind of belief which should be corrected.

4   KAMMA ON THE SOCIAL LEVEL

Kamma moves outwards

IN PRACTICAL terms it can be said that the human world is the world of intentional action. Human beings have a very sophisticated level of intention, which, in conjunction with their thought processes, allows them to achieve things which would be impossible for other animals. Although the lower animals, too, possess intention, it is limited to a nominal degree, being largely on the instinctual level.

Human thinking is guided by intention. Intention is what fashions the thinking process and, through that, external conditions. Our way of life, whether on the individual level or on the level of societies, both small and large, is directed by intention and the thinking process. It would not be wrong to say that intention, being the essence of *kamma,* is what decides our fate as human beings.

Now let us look at an example of how intention affects society. Intention on the negative side is that which is influenced by defilements. There are many kinds of defilements. When these defilements enter into our minds they colour the way we think. Here I will mention three kinds of defilements which play an important role in directing human behaviour. They are:

1. *Taṇhā* – craving for personal gain.
2. *Māna* – desire to dominate.
3. *Diṭṭhi* – clinging to views.

Normally when talking of defilements we tend to summarize them as greed, hatred and delusion, the roots of *akusala.* Greed, hatred and delusion are more or less defilements on the roots level. *Taṇhā, māna* and *diṭṭhi* are the active forms of defilements, or the roles they play in human undertakings. They are the form defilements most often take on the social level.

The way these three defilements direct human activities can be seen even more clearly on the social scale than on the individual level. When people's minds are ruled by the selfish desire for personal gain, aspiring to pleasures of the senses, their actions in society result in contention, deceit and exploitation. The laws and conventions formulated by society to control human behaviour are almost entirely necessitated by these things. And in spite of all efforts these problems seem to be almost impossible to solve.

A simple example is the drug problem. People have a tendency to be drawn towards addictive things, and there are a great number of people who are trapped in this problem. And why is it so hard to deal with? Primarily, because of the drug peddlers*. Their desire for the profit to be gained from the drug trade gives rise to the whole industry, and thus to the corruption, the gangs and so on. The industry has become so extensive and complex that any efforts to rectify the situation, including efforts to broadcast the dangers of drug abuse, are rendered ineffective. This problem of drug abuse, which is a problem on the social and national scale, arises from *tanha*.

Pollution is another case in point. When the indiscriminate dumping of chemicals and waste products presents a danger to the environment and public health, the government must create laws for the control of factories and waste disposal. But those running the industries are not inclined to give up their profits so easily. They find ways to evade or blatantly break the laws – in which case we find examples of government officials operating through selfishness. With minds dominated by greed and guided by selfishness, instead of carrying

---

* Those who are involved in the industry often try to justify themselves with the rationalisation that they are merely satisfying a demand, but Buddhism teaches awareness of Wrong Livelihood, the trade in things which will cause harm to other beings. This includes animals (for slaughter), slaves (which could include prostitutes), weapons, and drugs and alcohol. From the Buddhist perspective, the trader is not immune from blame for the damage caused by these things.

out the task expected of them, they take bribes. The law breakers go on unchecked, as does the pollution, causing strife for the whole of society. Both the presence of pollution, and the difficulty encountered in preventing and controlling it, arise from craving.

Corruption is another social problem which seems impossible to eradicate. This condition fans outwards to cause countless other problems in society, which are all in the end caused by craving. It is impossible to list all the problems caused by *taṇhā*.

Taṇhā also works in conjunction with *māna*, the craving for power and influence. From ancient times countries have fought and killed each other through this desire for power; sometimes at the instigation of one individual, sometimes through a faction, and sometimes collectively as whole countries. Coupled with the craving for personal gain, the craving for power gives rise to the exploitation, nationalism and expansionism in the world with all its subsequent chaos. You could say that the world turns almost entirely at the instigation of *taṇhā,* craving, and *māna,* pride. Human history is largely the story of these defilements.

The importance of *diṭṭhi* in the creation of *kamma*

However, if we look more deeply into the processes taking place, we will see that the defilement which exerts the most influence is the third one – *diṭṭhi*. *Diṭṭhi* is view or belief, the attachment to a certain way of thinking. The type of personal gain or power and influence aspired to are decided by ways of thinking. When there is the view that a certain condition is desirable and will provide true happiness, craving for personal gain is biased toward that end. Craving and pride generally play a supporting role to *diṭṭhi*. *Diṭṭhi* is therefore the most important and powerful of these three defilements.

The direction of society is decided by *diṭṭhi*. A sense of value of any given thing, either on an individual or social basis, is *diṭṭhi*. With this *diṭṭhi* as a basis, there follow the actions to realise the objects of desire. People's behaviour will be influenced accordingly.

For example, with the belief that happiness is to be found in the abundance of material goods, our actions and undertakings will tend to this end. This is a wrong view, thus the undertakings resulting from it will also be wrong. All attempts at so-called progress will be misguided and problem-ridden. Material progress thus brings problems in its wake. It is founded on two basically wrong and harmful views: 1. That humanity must conquer nature in order to achieve well-being and find true happiness; 2. That happiness is dependent on material wealth. These two views are the directors of the modern surge for progress.

Guided by wrong view, everything else will be wrong. With right view, actions are guided in the right direction. Thus, a desire for personal gain can be beneficial. But with wrong view or wrong belief all actions become harmful. On the individual level, this expresses itself in the belief in the desirability of certain conditions and the efforts to obtain them. Such action has *diṭṭhi* as its foundation. On the social level, we find the attitudes adhered to by whole societies. When there is a conviction in the desirability of any given thing, society praises and exalts it. This collective praise becomes a social value, a quality adhered to by society as a whole, which in turn pressures the members of the society to perpetuate such beliefs or preferences. It is easy to see the influence social values have on people. Sociologists and psychologists are very familiar with the role played by social values and the effect they have. From social values, beliefs extend outwards to become belief systems, ideologies, political and economic systems, such as capitalism, communism and so on, and religions. When theories, beliefs and political ideologies are blindly adhered to they are products of the defilement of *diṭṭhi*.

From one person these ideas fan out to become properties of whole groups and societies. One individual with wrong view can effect a whole society. A case in point is the country of Cambodia. One leader, guided by wrong view, desiring to change the social system of Cambodia, proceeded to try to realize his aim by authorizing the killing of millions of people and turning the whole country upside down*. Another example is the Nazis, who believed that the Jewish race was evil and had to be destroyed, and that the Aryan race were to be the masters of the world. From this belief arose all the atrocities which occurred during the Holocaust in World War II.

Then there are economic systems and ideologies, such as Communism and Consumerism: many of the changes that have taken place in the world over the last century have been based on belief in these ideologies. And now it seems that it was all somehow some kind of mistake! Eventually we have to turn around and undo the changes, which is another momentous upheaval for the population, as can be seen in Russia at the present time.

One of the ways in which *ditthi* causes problems on a social level is in the field of religion. When there is clinging to any view, human beings resort to exploitation and violence in the name of religion. Wars fought in the name of religion are particularly violent. This kind of clinging has thus been a great danger to mankind throughout history. The Buddha recognized the importance of *ditthi* and greatly emphasised it in his teaching. Even belief in religion is a form of *ditthi* which must be treated with caution in order to prevent it from becoming a blind attachment. Otherwise it can become a cause of persecution and violence. This is why the Buddha stressed the importance of *ditthi*, and urged circumspection in relation to it, as opposed to blind attachment**.

On the negative side, intention works through the various defilements, such as those mentioned just now. On the positive side we have the opposite kind of influences. When people's minds are

---

* Of course, that Pol Pot possessed such views was also largely due to external influences. Thus, external influences and individual action are intricately enmeshed. The *kamma* created in this instance would have been his conscious endorsement and wholehearted support of these views – See the section on external influences.

** In this context it is notable that religious wars have never been fought in the name of Buddhism, probably for the reasons given above.

guided by good qualities, the resulting events within society will take on a different direction. And so we have the attempts to rectify the problems in society and create good influences. Human society for this reason does not become completely destroyed. Sometimes human beings act through *mettā*, kindness, and *karuṇā*, compassion, giving rise to relief movements and human aid organizations. As soon as kindness enters into human awareness, human beings will undertake all sorts of works for the purpose of helping others.

International incidents, as well as relief movements, are motivated by intention, fashioned by either skilful or unskilful qualities, proceeding from mental *kamma* into verbal and bodily *kamma*. These institutions or organizations then proceed to either create or solve problems on the individual level, the group level, the social level, the national level, the international level and ultimately the global level.

The importance of *diṭṭhi*, whether as a personal view, a social value or an ideology, cannot be over-emphasised. The reader is invited to consider, for example, the results on society and the quality of life if even one social value, that of materialism, were to change into an appreciation of skilful action and inner well-being as the foundations for true happiness.

External influences and internal reflection

When people live together in any kind of group it is natural that they will influence each other. People are largely influenced by their environment. In Buddhism we call this *paratoghosa* – literally, the sound from outside, meaning the influence of external factors. *Paratoghosa* refers to external influences, or the social environment. These can be either harmful or beneficial. On the beneficial side, we have the *kalyāṇamitta**, the good friend. The good friend is one kind of external influence. The Buddha greatly

*The 'good friend' here is one who will guide one to betterment, who can teach the Dhamma, and thus refers to a teacher more than a friend as we normally understand the term

stressed the importance of a *kalyāṇamitta,* even going so far as to say that association with a *kalyāṇamitta* was the whole of the holy life *(brahmacariya).*

Most people are primarily influenced by *paratoghosa* of one kind or another. On the individual level this refers to the contact with others, the influence of which is obvious. Young children, for example, are readily influenced and guided by adults. On the larger scale, beliefs, social values, and the consensus of the majority serve the same function. People born into society are automatically exposed to and guided by these influences.

In general we can see that most people simply follow the influences from the social environment around them. An example is India in the time of the Buddha. At that time the Brahmanist religion completely controlled the social system, dividing the whole of society into four castes – the ruling caste, the intellectual or religious caste (the Brahmins), the merchant caste and the menial caste. This was the *status quo* for society at that time. Most people born into that society would naturally absorb and unquestioningly accept this state of affairs from the society around them.

But occasionally there arise those who dare to think for themselves. These are the ones who will initiate action to correct the problems in society by understanding how they come about. This is called the arising of *yoniso-manasikāra,* skilful reflection, which sees the mistaken practices adopted by society and looks for ways to improve them*, as did the Buddha in ancient India, seeing the fault of the caste system. The Buddha said that a person's real worth cannot be decided by his birth station, but by his actions, good or evil as the case may be. From the Buddha's skilful reflection, *yoniso-manasikāra,* a new teaching arose, which became the religion of Buddhism.

Without skilful reflection humanity would be utterly swamped

---

* *Yoniso-manasikāra* must be naturally founded on internal reflection. Thus it is not simply an intellectual consideration of social problems, but must be incorporated into the entire stream of Dhamma practice.

by the influence of external factors *(paratoghosa)* such as religious beliefs, traditions and social values. We can see how traditions and customs mould human attitudes. Most people are completely swayed by these things, and this is the *kamma* that they accumulate*. We could even say that traditions and customs are social *kamma* that has been accumulated through the ages, and these things in turn mould the beliefs and thoughts of the people within that society. These things are all social *kamma*.

Every once in a while there will be one who, gauging the social conventions and institutions of the time with *yoniso-manasikāra,* will instigate efforts to correct mistaken or detrimental beliefs and traditions. These means for dealing with problems will become new systems of thought, new social values and ways of life, which in turn become social currents with their own impetus. In fact these social currents are originated by individuals, and from there the masses follow. Thus we can say that society leads the individual, but at the same time, the individual is the originator of social values and conventions. Thus, in the final analysis, the individual is the important factor.

Personal responsibility in relation to social *kamma*

How does a socially accepted view become personal *kamma?* Personal *kamma* here arises at the point where the individual agrees to the values presented by society. Take, for example, the case of an autocrat who conceives a craving for power under the influence of *māna.* This is a condition arising within one person, but it spreads out to affect a whole society. In this case, what *kamma* does the society incur? Here, when the king or despot's advisers agree to and support his wishes, and when the people allow themselves to be caught up in the lust for greatness, this becomes

---

* The so-called 'silent majority' is thus not free of ethical responsibility. Such a silence, if accompanied by the resignation and acquiescence it usually generates, is in itself a condonement of social values and events, conditioned by the extent of apathy or lack of reflection involved.

kamma for those people also, and thus becomes *kamma* on a social scale. It may seem that this chain of events has arisen solely on account of one person, but this is not so. All are involved and all are kammically responsible, to a greater or lesser extent, depending on the extent of their personal involvement and their support. The views and desires conceived by the despot become adopted by the people around him. There is a conscious endorsement of that desire by the people. The craving for power and greatness thus spreads throughout the population and increases in intensity.

This agreement, or endorsement, of social values, is an intentional act on the level of each individual, which for most is done without skilful reflection. For instance, the concept of 'progress' so often spoken about in the present time is one based on certain assumptions. But most people do not enquire into the basic assumptions on which this concept is based. Thus the concept of 'progress' goes unchallenged. This lack of reflection is also a kind of *kamma,* as it leads to the submission to the social value concerned. Here in Thailand, we are accepting the social values introduced to us by the West. This has a marked influence on Thai society. Being exposed to this form of belief, the Thai people think that the material progress from the West is a good thing. Adopting this way of thinking, their whole way of life is affected, leading to a rejection of religion and a decline in morals.

It is not difficult to see the lack of reflection present in most people in society. Even to understand the workings of things on an elementary level, such as in seeing the cause and effect involved in personal actions, is beyond normal understanding. Most people follow the crowd. This is the way society usually operates, and this is social *kamma.*

All in all, contrary to the widespread image of Buddhism as a passive religion encouraging inaction, responsible social action is rather encouraged in the Buddha's teaching. There are numerous teachings given on factors encouraging social concord, such as the four *saṅgaha vatthu,* the Foundations for Social Unity: *dāna,* generosity; *piyavācā*, kindly speech; *atthacariyā*, helpful action; and *samānattatā*, impartiality or equal participation.

However, in Buddhism, all action should ideally arise from skilful mental qualities. A seemingly well-intentioned action can be ruined by the influence of unskilful mental states, such as anger or fear, or it can be tainted through ulterior motives. On the other hand, simply to cultivate skilful mental states without resultant social action is not very productive. So we can look at virtue on two levels: on the mental level we have, for example, the Four Sublime States.* These are the bases of altruistic action, or, at the least, of harmonious relations on a social level. On the second level we have the external manifestations of these skilful qualities, such as in the four *saṅgaha vatthu*, the Foundations of Unity. These two levels of virtue are interrelated.

The Four Sublime States are *mettā*, goodwill, friendliness; *karuṇā*, compassion, the desire to help other beings; *muditā*, sympathetic joy, gladness at the good fortune of others; and *upekkhā*, impartiality or equanimity.

Mettā, goodwill, is a mental stance assumed towards those who are in the normal condition, or on an equal plane with ourselves; *karuṇā*, compassion, is a proper mental attitude toward those who are in distress; *muditā*, sympathetic joy, is the attitude toward those who are experiencing success; *upekkhā*, equanimity or impartiality, is even-mindedness toward the various situations in which we find ourselves.

Now these four qualities, when looked at in practical terms, can be seen to manifest as the Four Foundations of Social Unity. *Dāna*, giving or generosity, is more or less a basic stance towards others in society, an attitude of generosity, which can be based on *mettā*, giving through goodwill; *karuṇā*, giving through compassion; or *muditā*, giving as an act of encouragement . Although this giving usually refers to material things, it can also be the giving of knowledge, labour and so on.

---

* *Brahmavihāra*

The second foundation of unity is *piyavācā*, kindly speech, which is usually based on the first three Sublime States. Friendly speech, based on *mettā*, as a basic attitude in everyday situations; kindly speech, based on *karuṇā*, in times of difficulty, as with words of advice or condolence; and congratulatory speech, based on *mudita*, as in words of encouragement in times of happiness and success. However, when confronted with problems in social situations, *piyavācā* can be expressed as impartial and just speech, based on *upekkhā*.

The third factor is *atthacariyā*, useful conduct, which refers to the volunteering of physical effort to help others. In the first factor, generosity, we had the giving of material goods. In the second factor, kindly speech, we have the offering of gentle speech. With this third item we have the offering of physical effort in the form of helpful conduct. This help can be on ordinary occasions, such as offering help in a situation where the recipient is not in any particular difficulty. Help in this instance is more or less a 'friendly gesture', thus is based on *mettā*, goodwill. Help can be offered in times of difficulty, in which case it is help based on *karuṇā*, compassion. Help can be offered as an encouragement in times of success, in which case it is based on *muditā*, sympathetic joy or gladness at the good fortune of others. Thus, *atthacariyā*, helpful conduct, may be based on any of these three Sublime States.

Finally we have *samānattatā*, literally, 'making oneself accessible or equal'. This is a difficult word to translate. It means to share with other people's pleasures and pains, to harmonize with them, to be one with them. It refers to sharing, cooperation and impartiality. We could say that it means to be humble, such as when helping others in their undertakings even if it is not one's duty, or to be fair, such as when arbitrating in a dispute.

In regards to Buddhism, therefore, while social action is encouraged, it should always stem from skilful mental states rather than idealist impulses. Any social action, no matter how seemingly worthwhile, will be ruined if it becomes tainted with unskilful intentions. For this reason, all action, whether individual or socially oriented, should be done carefully, with an awareness of the real intention behind it.

Here are some of the Buddha's words on *kamma* on the social level:

"At that time, the leaders among those beings came together. Having met, they conferred among themselves thus: 'Sirs! Bad doings have arisen among us, theft has come to be, slander has come to be, lies have come to be, the taking up of the staff has come to be. Enough! Let us choose one among us to admonish rightly those who should be admonished, to rebuke rightly those who should be rebuked, to banish rightly those who should be banished, and we will apportion some of our wheat to him.' With that, those beings proceeded to approach one being of fine attributes, more admirable, more inspiring and more awesome than any of the others, and said to him, 'Come, Sir, may you rightly admonish those who should be admonished, rightly rebuke those who should be rebuked, and rightly banish those who should be banished. We, in turn, will apportion some of our wheat to you.' Acknowledging the words of those other beings, he became their leader ... and there came to be the word 'king'*..."[30]

"In this way, *bhikkhus*, when the ruler of a country fails to apportion wealth to those in need, poverty becomes prevalent. Poverty being prevalent, theft becomes prevalent. Theft being prevalent, weapons become prevalent. When weapons become prevalent, killing and maiming become prevalent, lying becomes prevalent ... slander ... sexual infidelity ... abuse and frivolity ...covetousness and jealousy... wrong view becomes prevalent."[31]

---

* *Mahāsammata, lit.,* the Great Elect.

5 THE KAMMA
THAT ENDS KAMMA

IN THE LAST part of Chapter 1, four different kinds of *kamma* were mentioned, classified according to their relationships with their respective results:

1. Black *kamma*, black result.
2. White *kamma*, white result.
3. *Kamma* both black and white, result both black and white.
4. *Kamma* neither black nor white, result neither black nor white, this being the *kamma* that ends *kamma*.[32]

All of the varieties of *kamma*-results so far described have been limited to the first three categories, white *kamma*, black *kamma*, and both white and black *kamma*, or good *kamma* and bad *kamma*. The fourth kind of *kamma* remains to be explained. Because this fourth kind of *kamma* has an entirely different result from the first three, it has been given its own separate chapter.

Most people, including Buddhists, tend to be interested only in the first three kinds of *kamma*, completely disregarding the fourth.

Black, white and black-and-white *kamma* are generally described as the numerous kinds of action included within the ten bases of unskilful action*, such as killing living beings, infringing on the property of others, sexual misconduct, bad or malicious speech and so on, with their respective opposites as skilful actions. These kinds of *kamma* are determinants for various kinds of good and bad life experiences as has been explained above. The events of life in turn activate more good and bad *kamma*, thus spinning the

---

* See Chapter 1

wheel of *saṁsāra* round and round endlessly.

The fourth kind of *kamma* results in exactly the opposite way. Rather than causing the accumulation of more *kamma*, it leads to the cessation of *kamma*. In effect this refers to the practices which lead to the highest goal of Buddhism, Enlightenment, such as the **Noble Eightfold Path**, also known as the **Three-fold Training** (Moral Discipline, Mental Discipline and Wisdom), or the **Seven Factors of Enlightenment***. Sometimes this fourth kind of *kamma* is spoken of as the intention to abandon the other three kinds of *kamma*. Such intention is based on non-greed, non-hatred and non-delusion.

No discussion of *kamma* should fail to mention happiness and suffering. *Kamma* is the cause which results in happiness and suffering. As long as there is *kamma* there will be fluctuation between them. In aspiring to the highest good, however, devoid of every flaw, any condition tainted with either happiness or suffering, being subject to fluctuation, is inadequate. All worldly *kamma*, still tainted with suffering, is a cause of suffering.

However, this is valid only for the first three kinds of *kamma*. The fourth kind of *kamma* is exempt, because it leads to the cessation of *kamma*, and thus to the complete cessation of suffering. Although good *kamma* results in happiness, such happiness is tainted with suffering and can be a cause for suffering in the future. But this fourth kind of *kamma*, in addition to being in itself free of suffering, also gives rise to the untainted and total freedom from suffering. It is thus the purest kind of happiness.

The cessation or quenching of *kamma* was taught in a number of different religions in the Buddha's time, notably the Nigantha (Jain) Sect. The Niganthas taught the principle of old *kamma*, the cessation of *kamma*, and the mortification of the body in order to

---

* The Eight-fold Path: Right View, Right Intention, Right Speech, Right Action, Right Livelihood, Right Effort, Right Recollection and Right Concentration: The Seven Factors of Enlightenment: Recollection, Contemplation of Dhamma, Effort, Rapture, Tranquillity, Concentration and Equanimity.

'wear out' old *kamma*. If these three principles are not clearly distinguished from the Buddha's teaching they can easily be confused with it. Conversely, distinguishing them clearly from the principles of Buddhism can help to further clarify Buddhism's message. The Niganthas taught that:

"All happiness, suffering and neutral feeling are entirely caused by previous *kamma*. For this reason, when old *kamma* is done away with by practising austerities, and no new *kamma* is created, there will no longer be the influence of kamma-results. With no influence of kamma-results, *kamma* is done away with. *Kamma* being done away with, suffering is done away with. When suffering is done away with, feeling is done away with. With no more feeling, all suffering is completely quenched."[33]

The Niganthas believed that everything is caused by old *kamma*. To be free of suffering it is necessary to abandon old *kamma* and, by practising austerities, not accumulate new *kamma*. But Buddhism states that old *kamma* is merely one factor in the whole cause and effect process. This is an important point. Suffering is transcended through *kamma,* but it must be the right kind of *kamma,* the *kamma* which prevents the arising of *kamma* and thus leads to its cessation. Therefore, in order to nullify *kamma,* instead of merely stopping still or doing nothing, the practising Buddhist must be diligent in a practice based on right understanding. Correct practice induces independence, clarity and freedom from the directives of desire as it, in hand with ignorance, entangles beings in the search for attainments.

In order to clarify this fourth kind of *kamma,* its general features may be briefly summarized thus:

A. It is the path, or the practice, which leads to the cessation of *kamma*. At the same time, it is in itself a kind of *kamma.*

B. It is known as 'the *kamma* which is neither black nor white, having results which are neither black nor white, and which leads to the cessation of *kamma.*'

C. Non-greed, non-hatred and non-delusion are its root causes.

D. It is action based on wisdom and understanding, seeing the advantage and the inadequacy of things as they really are. It is thus the finest kind of action, action that is truly worthwhile, based on sound reason, and conducive to a healthy life.

E. Because this kind of action is not directed by desire, whether in the form of selfish exploitation, or inaction based on fear of personal loss, it is the most resolute and total kind of altruistic effort, guided and supported by mindfulness and wisdom.

F. It is *kusala kamma,* skilful action, on the level known as Transcendent Skilful Action* (in the commentaries known as *magga cetanā,* the intention pertaining to the Path; or *maggañāṇa,* insight pertaining to the Path).

G. In terms of practice, it can be called the Eight-fold Path to the cessation of suffering, the Fourth of the Four Noble Truths; the Seven Factors of Enlightenment, or the Three-fold Training, depending on the context; it is also referred to in a general sense as the intention to abandon the first three kinds of *kamma.*

In regard to point E. above, it is noteworthy that *taṇhā,* or desire, is seen by most people as the force which motivates action. The more desire there is, the more intense and competitive is the resultant action. If there were no desire there would be no incentive to act, people would become inert and lazy. This kind of understanding comes from looking at human nature only partially. If used as a guide-line for practice it can cause untold problems, on both the individual and social levels.

In fact, desire is an impetus for both action and inaction. When it is searching for objects with which to feed itself, desire is an impetus for action. This kind of action tends to generate exploitation and conflict, self-seeking at the expense of others. However, at a time when good and altruistic actions are called for, desire will become an incentive to inaction, binding the self to personal comfort, even if only attachment to sleep. Thus it becomes an encumbrance or stumbling block to performing good deeds. If

* *Lokuttara Kusala Kamma*

ignorance is still strong, that is, there is no understanding of the value of good actions, desire will encourage inertia and negligence. For this reason, desire may be an incentive for either an exploitive kind of activity, or a lethargic kind of inactivity, depending on the direction it takes.

The conduct which supports a healthy life and is truly beneficial is completely different from this pandering to selfish desires, and in many cases calls for a relinquishment of personal comforts and pleasures. This kind of action can therefore not be achieved through desire (except if we first qualify our terms), but must be achieved through an understanding and appreciation of the advantage of such practice as it really is.

This appreciation, or aspiration, is called in Pali **chanda*** (known in full as *kusalachanda* or *Dhammachanda*). *Chanda* is the real incentive for any truly constructive actions. However, *chanda* may be blocked or weighed down by desire as it attaches to laziness, lethargy, or personal comfort. In this case, desire will stain any attempts to perform good actions with suffering, by resisting the practice through these negative states. If there is clear understanding of the advantage of those actions and sufficient appreciation *(chanda)* of them, enabling the burdening effect of desire to be overcome, *chanda* becomes, in addition to an impetus for action, a cause for happiness also. This kind of happiness differs from the happiness resulting from desire – it is radiant and spacious rather than shallow and dull, conducive to creative and useful activities free of suffering. In this case, *samādhi,* the firmly established mind, comprising effort, mindfulness and understanding, will develop within and directly support such undertakings. This kind of practice is known as 'the *kamma* that ends *kamma.'*

By practising according to the Noble Eight-fold Path desire has no channel through which to function, and is eliminated.

---

* *Chanda* literally means 'desire', or 'satisfaction', but when prefixed by 'kusala' or 'Dhamma', it refers to a skilful kind of desire. In general usage, however, it is sometimes rendered simply as 'chanda', the prefixes more or less understood.

Greed, hatred and delusion do not arise. With no desire, greed, hatred or delusion, there is no *kamma*. With no *kamma* there are no kamma-results to bind the mind. With no *kamma* to bind the mind, there emerges a state of clarity which transcends suffering. The mind which was once a slave of desire becomes one that is guided by wisdom, directing actions independently of desire's influence.

Here follow some of the Buddha's words dealing with the *kamma* that ends *kamma*:

"**Bhikkhus**, know *kamma*, know the cause of *kamma*, know the variations of *kamma*, know the results of *kamma*, know the cessation of *kamma* and know the way leading to the cessation of *kamma* ... **Bhikkhus**, intention, I say, is *kamma*. A person intends before acting through body, speech or mind. What is the cause of *kamma*? Contact* *(phassa)* is the cause of *kamma*. What are the variations of *kamma*? They are, the *kamma* which results in birth in hell, the *kamma* which results in birth in the animal world, the *kamma* which results in birth in the realm of hungry ghosts, the *kamma* which results in birth in the human realm, and the *kamma* which results in birth in the heaven realms. These are known as the variations of *kamma*. What are the results of *kamma*? I teach three kinds of kamma-result. They are, results in the present time, results in the next life, or results in a future life. These I call the results of *kamma*. What is the cessation of *kamma*? With the cessation of contact, *kamma* ceases**. This very Noble Eightfold Path is the way leading to the cessation of *kamma*. That is, Right View, Right Intention, Right Speech, Right Action, Right Livelihood, Right Effort, Right Mindfulness and Right concentration."[34]

---

* That is to say, contact through the senses of eye, ear, nose, tongue, body and mind.
** Cessation here refers to the cessation of the cycle of conditioning generated by Avijjā, ignorance. – The Author.

"Bhikkhus, when a noble disciple thus clearly understands *kamma,* the cause of *kamma,* the variations of *kamma,* the results of *kamma,* the cessation of *kamma* and the way leading to the cessation of *kamma,* he then clearly knows the Holy Life *(brahmacariya)* comprising keen wisdom, which is the cessation of this *kamma."* [34]

"Bhikkhus, I will expound new *kamma,* old *kamma,* the cessation of *kamma* and the way leading to the cessation of *kamma* ... What is old *kamma?* Eye ... ear ... nose ... tongue ... body ... mind should be understood as old *kamma,* these being formed from conditions, born of volition, and the base of feeling. This is called *'old kamma'.*

"Bhikkhus, what is *'new kamma'?* Actions created through body, speech and mind in the present moment, these are called *'new kamma'.*

"Bhikkhus, what is the cessation of *kamma?* The experience of liberation arising from the cessation of bodily *kamma,* verbal *kamma* and mental *kamma,* is called the cessation of *kamma.*

"Bhikkhus, what is the way leading to the cessation of *kamma?* This is the Noble Eight-fold Path, namely, Right View ... Right Concentration. This is called the way leading to the cessation of *kamma."* [35]

"Bhikkhus, this body does not belong to you, nor does it belong to another. You should see it as old *kamma,* formed by conditions, born of volition, a base of feeling." [36]

"Bhikkhus, these three *kamma-* origins, greed, hatred and delusion, are causes of *kamma.* Whatever *kamma* is performed on account of greed, is born from greed, has greed as origin, and is formed from greed, results in rebirth. Wherever his *kamma* ripens, there the doer must experience the fruits of his *kamma,* be it in the present life, in the next life or in a future life. *Kamma* performed on account of hatred ... *kamma* performed on account of delusion ...(the same as for greed)

"*Bhikkhus,* these three *kamma*-origins, non-greed, non-hatred and non-delusion, are causes of *kamma.* Whatever *kamma* is performed on account of non-greed, is born from non-greed, has non-greed as origin, and is formed from non-greed, is devoid of greed, that *kamma* is given up, cut off at the root, made like a palm tree stump, completely cut off with no possibility of arising again. Whatever *kamma* is performed on account of non-hatred ... on account of non-delusion ... [37]

"*Bhikkhus,* these three *kamma*-origins, greed, hatred and delusion, are causes of *kamma.* Whatever *kamma* is performed on account of greed, is born from greed, has greed as origin, is formed from greed, that *kamma* is unskilful ... is harmful ... has suffering as a result. That *kamma* exists for the arising of more *kamma,* not for the cessation of *kamma.* Whatever *kamma* is done on account of hatred ... on account of delusion ...

"*Bhikkhus,* these three *kamma*-origins, non-greed, non-hatred and non-delusion, are causes of *kamma.* Whatever *kamma* is done on account of non-greed, is born of non-greed, has non-greed as origin, is formed from non-greed, that *kamma* is skilful ... not harmful ... has happiness as a result. That *kamma* leads to the cessation of *kamma,* not to the arising of *kamma.* Whatever *kamma* is done on account of non-hatred ... on account of non-delusion ..." [38]

"*Bhikkhus,* killing of living beings, I say, is of three kinds. That is, with greed as motive, with hatred as motive and with delusion as motive. Stealing ... sexual misconduct ... lying ... malicious tale-bearing ... abusive speech ... frivolous speech ... covetousness ... resentment ... wrong view, I say, are of three kinds. They are, with greed as motive, with hatred as motive and with delusion as motive. For this reason, greed is a cause for *kamma,* hatred is a cause for *kamma,* delusion is a cause for *kamma.* With the cessation of greed, there is the cessation of a cause of *kamma.* With the cessation of hatred, there is the cessation of a cause of *kamma*. With the cessation of delusion, there is the cessation of a cause of *kamma.*"[39]

"*Bhikkhus,* there are these four *kammas* ... What is black *kamma,* black result? Some people in this world are given to killing, given to stealing, given to sexual misconduct, given to lying, given to drinking intoxicants which lead to heedlessness. This is called black *kamma,* black result.

"*Bhikkhus,* what is white *kamma,* white result? Some people in this world dwell aloof from killing, aloof from stealing, aloof from sexual misconduct, aloof from lying, aloof from the drinking of intoxicants which lead to heedlessness. This is called white *kamma,* white result.

"*Bhikkhus,* what is *kamma* both back and white with result both black and white? Some people in this world create actions through body ... speech ... mind which are both harmful and not harmful. This is called '*kamma* both black and white with result both black and white'.

"*Bhikkhus,* what is *kamma* neither black nor white with result neither black nor white, which leads to the cessation of *kamma?* Within those three kinds of *kamma,* the intention to abandon (those kinds of *kamma*), this is called the *kamma* which is neither black nor white, with result neither black nor white, which leads to the ending of *kamma.*"[40]

"Listen, Udayi. A *bhikkhu* in this Teaching and Discipline cultivates the Mindfulness Enlightenment Factor ... the Equanimity Enlightenment Factor, which tend to seclusion, tend to dispassion, tend to cessation, which are well developed, which are boundless, void of irritation. Having cultivated the Mindfulness Enlightenment Factor ... the Equanimity Enlightenment Factor... desire is discarded. With the discarding of desire, *kamma* is discarded. With the discarding of *kamma,* suffering is discarded. Because of this, with the ending of desire there is the ending of *kamma;* with the ending of *kamma* there is the ending of suffering."[41]

6 MISUNDERSTANDINGS OF THE LAW OF KAMMA

Who causes happiness and suffering?

ACCORDING to the Buddha's words, "Through Ignorance, bodily actions ... verbal actions ... mental actions ... are created, of one's own accord ... through external influences ... knowingly ... unknowingly." There are also instances where the Buddha refuted both the theory that all happiness and suffering are caused by the self (known as *Attakāravāda)* and the theory that all happiness and suffering are caused by external forces (known as *Pārakāravāda).* This highlights the need to see *kamma* in its relation to the whole stream of cause and effect. The extent of any involvement, either one's own or externally, must be considered in relation to this process. Otherwise the common misunderstanding arises that all events are caused by personal actions to the exclusion of everything else.

What must be grasped is the difference between *kamma* in the context of natural law, and *kamma* in the context of ethics. When speaking of *kamma* as a natural law, a process that exists in nature and incorporates a wide range of conditioning factors, we do not need to over-emphasize the role of individual action. But on the level of ethics, the teaching of *kamma* is meant to be put into actual practice in everyday life. Consequently, in terms of the individual, full responsibility must be taken for all intentional actions. This is emphasised in the Buddha's words from the Dhammapada*, **'Be a refuge unto yourself.'**

In addition to meaning that the individual must help and act

---

* The *Dhammapada,* composed in a singularly simple and straight-forward style, is one of the oldest and most popular sections of the Pali Canon, containing a collection of stanzas attributed to the Buddha himself.

for himself, this injunction also includes our relationship when helped by other people. That is, even in the event of help arising from external sources, the recipient is still responsible for accepting such help on all or any of the following three levels: a) In the invitation, whether intentional or otherwise, whether conscious or not, of such help; b) In fostering such help through appropriate behaviour; c) And at the very least, in the acceptance of such help. For this reason, the principle of *kamma* on the level of natural law and on the level of ethics do not conflict, but actually support each other.

Beliefs which are contrary to the law of *kamma*

There are three philosophies which are considered by Buddhism to be wrong view and which must be carefully distinguished from the teaching of *kamma* –

1. *Pubbekatahetuvāda* or *Pubbekatavāda*: The belief that all happiness and suffering arise from previous *kamma* (Past-action determinism).

2. *Issaranimmānahetuvāda*: The belief that all happiness and suffering are caused by the creation of a Supreme Being (Theistic determinism).

3. *Ahetu-apaccayavāda*, or *Ahetuvāda*: The belief that all happiness and suffering are random, having no cause (Indeterminism or Accidentalism)*.

Concerning this, we have the Buddha's words:

"Bhikkhus, these three sects, on being questioned by the wise, fall back on tradition and stand fast on inaction (akiriyā). They are:

1. The group of ascetics or Brahmins which teaches and is of the view that all happiness, suffering and neutral feeling are entirely a result of *kamma* done in a previous time

---

* These last two beliefs are good examples of two tacitly but widely-accepted views in the modern world, while the first is one misunderstanding of *kamma* commonly found in Buddhist and Hindu societies.

(Pubbekatahetu).

2. The group of ascetics and Brahmins which teaches and is of the view that all happiness, suffering and neutral feeling are entirely a result of the will of a Supreme Being. *(Issaranimmānahetu).*

3. The group of ascetics and Brahmins which teaches and is of the view that all happiness, suffering and neutral feeling are entirely without cause *(ahetu apaccaya).*

"*Bhikkhus*, of those three groups of ascetics and Brahmins, I approach the first group and ask, 'I hear that you uphold this teaching and view ... Is that so?' If those ascetics and Brahmins, on being thus questioned by me, answer that it is true, then I say to them, 'If that is so, then you have killed living beings as a result of *kamma* committed in a previous time, have stolen as a result of *kamma* done at a previous time, have engaged in sexual misconduct ... have uttered false speech ... have held wrong view as a result of *kamma* done in a previous time.'

"*Bhikkhus*, adhering to previously done *kamma* as the essence, there are neither motivation nor effort with what should be done and what should not be done ... Not upholding ardently what should be done and not abandoning what should be abandoned, then those ascetics and Brahmins are as if deluded, lacking a control, incapable of having any true teaching. This is our legitimate refutation of the first group of ascetics and Brahmins holding these views."

"*Bhikkhus*, of those three groups of ascetics and Brahmins, I approach the second group ... and say to them, 'If that is so, then you have killed living beings because of the directives of a Supreme Being ... stolen the goods of others ... engaged in sexual misconduct ... uttered false speech ... have held wrong view because of the directives of a Supreme Being."

"*Bhikkhus*, adhering to the will of a Supreme Being as the essence, there are neither motivation nor effort with what should be done and what should not be done ..."

"Bhikkhus, of those groups of ascetics and Brahmins, I approach the third ... and say to them, 'If that is so, then you have killed living beings for no reason whatsoever ... stolen the things of others ... engaged in sexual misconduct ... uttered false speech ... have held wrong view for no reason whatsoever.'

"Bhikkhus, adhering to accidentalism as being the essence, there are neither motivation nor effort with what should be done and what should not be done ..."[42]

The first of these three schools of thought is that of the Niganthas, about which we can learn some more from the Buddha's words:

"Bhikkhus, there are some ascetics and Brahmins who are of this view, 'All happiness and suffering are entirely caused by previous *kamma*. For this reason, with the suppression of old *kamma* through austerities, there will be no influence exerted by *kamma* results. When there is no more influence of *kamma* results, *kamma* is ended. With the ending of *kamma* there is an ending of suffering. With the ending of suffering there is an ending of feeling. With the ending of feeling, all suffering is eventually extinguished. *Bhikkhus*, the Niganthas are of this view."[43]

The following words from the Buddha clearly illustrate the Buddhist view:

"Listen, *Sivaka*. Some kinds of feeling arise with bile as condition ... with changes in the weather as condition ... with inconstant behaviour as condition ... with danger from an external source as condition ... with *kamma*-results as condition. Any ascetic or Brahmin who is of the view that, 'All feeling is entirely caused by previous *kamma*', I say is mistaken."[44]

These words discourage us from going too far with *kamma*, considering it as entirely a thing of the past. Such a view encourages inactivity, a passive waiting for the results of old *kamma* to ripen, taking things as they come without thinking to correct or improve them. This is a harmful form of wrong view, as can be seen from the Buddha's words above.

Significantly, in the words given above, the Buddha asserts effort and motivation as the crucial factors in deciding the ethical value of these various teachings on *kamma.*

The Buddha did not dismiss the importance of previous *kamma,* because previous *kamma* does play a part in the cause and effect process, and thus has an effect on the present in its capacity as one of the conditioning factors. But it is simply one of those conditions, it is not a super-natural force to be clung to or submitted to passively. An understanding of the *Paṭiccasamuppāda* and the cause and effect process will clarify this.

For example, if a man climbs to the third floor of a building, it is undeniably true that his arriving is a result of past action, that is, walking up the stairs. And having arrived there, it is impossible for him to reach out and touch the ground with his hand, or drive a car up and down there. Obviously this is because he has gone up to the third floor. Or, having arrived at the third floor, whether he is too exhausted to continue is also related to having walked up the stairs. His arrival there, the things he is able to do there and the situations he is likely to encounter, are all certainly related to the 'old *kamma*' of having walked up the stairs. But exactly which actions he will perform, his reactions to the situations which arise there, whether he will take a rest, walk on, or walk back down the stairs and out of that building, are all matters which he can decide for himself in that present moment, for which he will also reap the results. Even though the action of walking up the stairs may still be influencing him (for example, with his strength sapped he may be unable to function efficiently in any given situation), whether he decides to give in to that tiredness or try to overcome it are all matters which he can decide for himself in the present moment.

Therefore, old *kamma* should be understood in its relation to the whole cause and effect process. In terms of ethical practice, to understand the cause and effect process is to be able to learn from old *kamma,* understanding the situation at hand, and to skilfully make a plan of action for improving and correcting the future.

Can *kamma* be erased?

At one time the Buddha said, "*Bhikkhus,* there are those who say 'Whatever *kamma* is made by this man, he will receive identical results thereof.' If such were the case, there could be no higher life (*brahmacariya*), no path could be perceived for the successful ending of suffering*."

"But with the view, 'When *kamma* based on a certain kind of feeling is made (pleasant or unpleasant, for example), results arise in conformity with that feeling,' the higher life can be, there is a way for the ending of suffering."

"*Bhikkhus,* for some people, only a little bad *kamma* can lead to rebirth in hell, but for others that same small amount of bad *kamma* will produce results only in the present moment, and even then, only the most extreme aspects of it will become apparent, not the minor.

"What kind of person is it who, for only a little bad *kamma,* goes to hell? There are those who have not trained their actions, have not trained in *sīla,* have not trained their minds and have not developed wisdom. They are of little worth, are of small status and dwell discontented over minor *kamma* results. This kind of person it is who, over just a little bad *kamma,* can go to hell (like putting a lump of salt into a very small vessel).

"What kind of person is it who, for exactly the same amount of bad *kamma,* receives fruit only in the present, and even then, the minor aspects of that *kamma* do not manifest, only the major? There are those who have trained their actions, have trained in *sīla,* have trained their minds and have developed wisdom. They are not of little worth, they are great beings, they have a measureless abiding. For this kind of person, just the same kind of minor bad *kamma* gives results only in the present,

---

*This belief is illustrated in the commonly held belief that if you break down a termite mound, for example, in this life, in a future life you must inevitably have your house broken down by those termites, possibly reborn as human beings.

and even then the minor aspects of that *kamma* do not manifest, only the major (like putting a lump of salt into a river)."[45]

"Listen, householder, some teachers give the teaching and are of the view that those who kill living beings must without exception go to the woeful states, falling to hell; that those who steal must without exception go to the woeful states, falling to hell; that those who commit adultery must without exception go to the woeful states, falling to hell; that those who lie must without exception go to the woeful states, falling to hell. Disciples of those teachers, thinking, 'Our teacher gives the teaching and is of the view that those who kill living beings must all fall into hell,' conceive the view thus, 'I have killed living beings. Therefore I too must go to hell.' Not relinquishing that speech and that view, he indeed goes to hell, just as if pushed there by force.

"As for the *Tathāgata**, fully enlightened Buddha, he arises in the world ... He speaks in dispraise of killing living beings ... stealing ... adultery ... lying, in many ways, and teaches, 'Killing of living beings ... stealing ... adultery ... lying should be abandoned'. A disciple of the Teacher, reflecting thus, 'The Blessed One speaks in dispraise of killing living beings ... in many a way, and teaches the abandoning of killing living beings. I have killed many beings already. That killing of living beings by me is not good, is not worthy. I will suffer on account of those actions, and on their account I will not be beyond reproof.' Reflecting in this way, he gives up killing of living beings, and is one who abandons the killing of living beings from that time on. Thus does he abandon that bad *kamma* ...

"He abandons the killing of living beings ... lying ... malicious tale-bearing ... coarse speech ... frivolous speech ... covetousness ... enmity ... wrong view. He is one endowed with Right View, he is a Noble Disciple with a mind free of greed, free

---

* *Tathāgata:* The 'thus-gone one', a name often used by the Buddha when referring to himself.

of aversion, not deluded but possessed of self awareness and firm mindfulness. He dwells with a mind full of goodwill, spreading to the first ... second ... third ... the whole four directions, above, below, spreading out wide to the whole world, to all beings in all places, with a mind full of goodwill that is expansive, grand, boundless, free of enmity and ill will. Having so thoroughly developed the Mind Deliverance through Goodwill, any moderate amount of *kamma* previously done will no longer manifest ..."[46]

These words have been quoted to prevent misunderstandings in relation to the fruition of *kamma*. The present extract is only a small portion of the material available, as to present it all would take up too much space.

Do *kamma* and not-self contradict each other?

There is one question which, though only occasionally asked, tends to linger in the minds of many newcomers to the study of Buddhism: "Do the teachings of *kamma* and not-self contradict each other?" If everything, including body and mind, is not-self, then how can there be *kamma?* Who is it who commits *kamma?* Who receives the results of *kamma?* These doubts are not simply a phenomenon of the present time, but have existed from the time of the Buddha, as can be seen in the following example:

A *bhikkhu* conceived the following doubt,

"We know that body, feeling, perception, volitional activities and consciousness* are not self. If so, then who is it who receives the results of the *kamma* made by this 'non-self'?"

At that time, the Blessed One, knowing the thoughts of that *bhikkhu,* addressed the *bhikkhus* thus:

"Bhikkhus, it may be that some foolish people in this Teaching and Discipline, with mind fallen into Ignorance and confused by desire, might conceive the teaching of the Master

---

* *Rūpa, vedanā, saññā, saṅkhāra* and *viññāṇa:* the Five *Khandhas.*

to be rationalized thus: 'We know that body, feeling, perception, volitional activities and consciousness are not self. If that is so, who is it who receives the results of the *kamma* created by this 'non-self'?' All of you now, having been thoroughly instructed by me, consider these matters: is form permanent or impermanent?" *"Impermanent, Venerable Sir."* "Is what is impermanent (a cause for) happiness or suffering?" *"Suffering, Venerable Sir."* "Of that which is impermanent, unsatisfactory, and normally subject to degeneration, is it proper to say that 'this is mine, this is me, this is my self.'?" *"No, it is not proper, Venerable Sir."* "For that reason, form, feeling, perception, volitional activities and consciousness, of whatever description, are merely form, feeling, perception, volitional activities and consciousness. They are not 'mine', not 'me', not 'my self'. Reflect on this thus as it is with right wisdom. The learned, Noble Disciple, seeing in this way, does not attach to form, feeling, perception, volitional activities or consciousness. He is free of those things, and has no further task to do." [47]

Before examining this scriptural reference, consider the following illustration: Suppose both the reader and the author are standing on the bank of a river, watching the water flow by. The water flows in a mostly flat area, therefore it flows very slowly. The earth in that particular area is red, which gives this body of water a reddish tint. In addition to this, the water passes many heavily populated areas, from where people have long thrown refuse in, which, in addition to the industrial waste poured into the water by a number of recently built factories, pollutes the water. The water is therefore uninhabitable for most animals. There are not many fish, shrimps and so forth. In a word, the body of water we are looking at is reddish, dirty, polluted, sparsely inhabited and sluggish. All of these features together are the characteristics of this particular body of water. Some of these characteristics might be similar to other streams or rivers, but the sum total of these characteristics is unique to this stream of water.

Presently we are informed that this body of water is called the Tah Wung River. Different people describe it in different ways. Some say the Tah Wung River is dirty and doesn't have many fish. Some say the Tah Wung River flows very slowly. Some say that the Tah Wung River is red-coloured.

Standing on the river's bank, it seems to us that the body of water we are looking at is actually complete in itself. Its attributes, such as being sluggish, red-coloured, dirty, and so on, are all caused by various conditioning factors, such as the flowing water contacting the red earth. In addition, the water which we are looking at is constantly flowing by. The water which we saw at first is no longer here, and the water we are now seeing will quickly pass. Even so, the river has its unique features, which do not change as long as the relevant conditioning factors have not changed.

But we are told, then, that this is the Tah Wung River. Not only that, they say that the Tah Wung River is sluggish, dirty, and short of fish. With a glance, we can see no 'Tah Wung River' other than this body of water flowing by. We can see no 'Tah Wung River' possessing this body of water. In addition, they tell us that the Tah Wung River breaks up the red earth as it passes, which makes the water turn red. It's almost as if this 'Tah Wung River' does something to the red earth, which causes the red earth to 'punish' it by turning its water red.

We can see clearly that this body of water is subject to the process of cause and effect governed by its various conditioning factors; the water splashing against the red earth and the red earth dissolving into the water is one causal condition, the result of which is the red-coloured water. We can find no 'body' doing anything or receiving any results. We can see no actual Tah Wung River anywhere. The water flowing past us now flows right on by, the water seen previously is no longer here. New water is constantly taking its place. We are able to define that body of water only by describing its conditioning factors and the events which arise as a result, causing the features we have observed. If there was an actual and unchanging Tah Wung River, it would be impossible for that flow of water to proceed according to its various determining factors. Finally we see that this 'Tah Wung River' is superfluous. We can speak about that body of water without having to bother with this 'Tah Wung River'. In actual fact there is no Tah Wung River at all!

As time goes by we travel to a new district. Wishing to describe the body of water we saw at that time to the people there, we find ourselves at a loss. Then we recall someone telling us that that body of water was known as the Tah Wung River. Knowing this, we can relate our experience fluently, and the other people are able to listen with interest and attention. We tell them that the Tah Wung River has dirty water, not many fish, is sluggish, and that the Tah Wung River is red-coloured.

At that time, we realize clearly that this 'Tah Wung River', and the role it plays in the events we describe, are simply conventions of language used for convenience in communication. Whether the convention of Tah Wung River exists or not, and whether we use it or not, has no bearing whatsoever on the actions of that body of water. That body of water continues to be a process of inter-related cause and effect reactions. We can clearly distinguish between the convention and the actual condition. Now we are able to understand and use the convention of speech with ease.

The things which we conventionally know as people, to which we give names, and refer to as 'me' and 'you', are in reality continuous and inter-connected streams of events, made up of countless related constituent factors, just like that river. They are subject to countless events, directed by related determinants, both from within that stream of events and from without. When a particular reaction takes place in a causal way, the fruit of that action arises, causing changes within the flow of events.

The conditions which we refer to as *kamma* and *vipāka*, are simply the play of cause and effect within one particular stream of events. They are perfectly capable of functioning within that stream without the need for the conventions of name, or the words 'me' and 'you', either as owners or perpetrators of those actions, or as receivers of their results. This is reality*, which functions naturally in this way. But for convenience in communication within the social world, we must use the convention of names for particular streams of events, such as Mr. Smith and so on.

Having accepted the convention, we must accept responsibility for that stream of events, becoming the owner, the active perpetrator and the passive subject of actions and their results, as the case may be. But whether we use these conventions or not, whether we accept the labels or not, the stream of events itself functions anyway, directed by cause and effect. The important point is to be aware of things as they are, distinguishing between the convention and the condition itself. One and the same thing, in the context of its actual nature, is spoken of in one way, but when spoken of in conventional terms it must be referred to in another way. If we have an understanding of the actual reality of these things we will not be deluded or confused by them.

Both the reality and the convention are inevitable. The reality (often referred to as *Paramattha)* is the natural condition. Conventions are a useful and practical human invention. Problems arise when human beings confuse the two things, clinging to the reality and trying to make it follow conventions. Within the actual reality there is no confusion, because the principle naturally functions by itself, not being subject to man's ideas about it – it is people who become confused. And because reality is not confused, functioning independently of people's desires, it frustrates their desires and makes them even more confused and frustrated. Any problem occurring is purely a human one.

As can be seen in the quotation above, the *bhikkhu* who conceived this doubt was confusing the description of the reality,

---

*The word 'reality' might seem somewhat arbitrary. In the context of this work, we could define it more clearly as 'the natural world as distinct from human conventional appendages.'

·which he had learnt, with the convention, to which he still clung. This was the cause of his bewilderment and doubt. If we retain the original wording, it goes something like this: "If *kamma* is created by not-self, what self is it that receives the fruits of *kamma?*" The first part of the sentence is spoken according to his acquired knowledge of the reality, while the second part is spoken according to his own habitual perception. Naturally they don't fit.

From what has been given here, we can summarize thus:

– The teachings of Not-self and *kamma* are not at all contradictory. On the contrary, not-self gives weight to the teaching of *kamma*. Because things are not-self, there can be *kamma,* and *kamma* can function. When the process of events is operating, all the factors involved must arise, cease and interact unhindered, so that the stream of events can proceed. There can be no permanent or actual entity to block the flow. **If there was a self, there could be no *kamma,* because a self (by definition) is not subject to cause and effect.** Nothing can effect its existence, or cause the self to be other than what it is. In the end we would have to divide the individual into two levels, such as is held by the *Sassataditthi* (belief in an intrinsic self) sects, who believe that the self who creates and receives the fruits of *kamma* is merely the external or superficial self, while the real self, or essence of the self, lies unchanging within.

– The creation of *kamma* and its results in the present time is done without the need for an agent or a recipient. We should consider thus: 'Which factors are operating here? What relationships are involved? What events are arising within the stream as a result, and how are they effecting changes within the stream?' When a cause, known as *kamma,* or action, arises, there follows the result, known as *vipāka,* within that stream of events. We call this 'cause and effect'. This process is not dependent on an owner of those actions, or a doer and a recipient of results as an additional, extraneous entity. *Kamma* is the flow of cause and effect within that stream of events, unlike the conventions which are pasted over them. When there is an agreement to call that stream of events Mr. Smith or Miss Brown, there arises an owner of actions, a doer and a recipient of results. However, the stream of events proceeds regardless, completely perfect within itself as far as the cause and effect process goes. It does not depend on names in order to function. When it is time to speak in the context of a stream of events, describing its operation, its causes and its results, then we can so speak. When it is time to speak in the context of conventions, describing actions and the fruits of actions in personal terms, we can speak thus also. If we do not cling to these things or confuse them, then we will have the right understanding.

Even with regard to inanimate objects, such as the river above, most people still manage to cling to conventions as actual entities. How much more so when it comes to human beings, which are more complex and intricate junctions of causal processes, involving mental factors. As for these mental factors, they are extremely intricate. Even impermanence is incomprehensible to most people. There are those who remark, for instance, "Who says memory is impermanent and unstable? Memory is permanent, because wherever and whenever it arises, it is always memory, it never changes."

Some people may agree with this statement, but if the argument is applied to a material object the error becomes more apparent. The argument given above is comparable to saying, "Who says the body is impermanent? The body is permanent and unchanging, because wherever and whenever the body arises, it is always the body, it never changes." It is easier to see the mistake in this latter argument, but actually both arguments are equally mistaken. That is, both confuse memory, for instance, and the label 'memory', or body and the label 'body'. The arguments suggest that memory and the body are stable and unchanging, but in fact what they are saying is that the names 'memory' and 'body' are (relatively) stable and unchanging.

Studying the Law of *Kamma* solely on the level of convention sometimes leads to a simplistic view of things. For instance, assuming that Mr. Smith, having committed such-and-such *kamma,* on such-and-such a day, ten years later receives such-and-such bad result. The cause and effect process referred to jumps over a span of ten years all in one step. This makes it difficult to carefully consider the real process involved, because the total stream of events involved is not taken into account. Studying the same case in terms of the natural stream of events helps to see the operation of cause and effect relationships more completely and in more detail, revealing the real significance of the results which have arisen and how they have come about.

Suppose a certain Mr. Brown has an argument with his neighbour and kills him. Although he goes into hiding, eventually he is arrested and convicted. Later, even after having been freed at the end of his prison term, Mr. Brown still experiences remorse on account of his evil actions. He is often haunted by the image of the murder victim. His facial features and physical bearing change, exhibiting agitation, fear and depression. These mental states, coupled with his strong physical bearing, together cause him to become even more violent and bad-tempered. As time goes on his physical features take on coarse and hostile characteristics. He hides his suffering by aggressive behaviour, becoming a danger to society and to himself, unable to find any real happiness.

In this example, we can say simply that Mr. Brown has committed bad *kamma* and suffered the results of his actions. This is the normal way of speaking*, which is readily understood by most people. This is called 'speaking in terms of convention'. It is a way of communication, facilitating the exchange of ideas, but it speaks merely of the external appearance of things, or the grosser results of the relevant factors which are concealed within. It does not pierce the true essence of the matter, of the inter-related factors reacting according to the natural laws.

However, if we speak in terms of reality, we can speak of the essence in its entirety, referring to it as a process of events. For

---

* – For Buddhists, that is.

example, we could say that within the operation of this set of Five *Khandhas,* a mind state based on anger arose. There followed the mental proliferation in accord with that anger, leading to physical action. The mind, conceiving in this way, began to change, taking on hostile attributes, such as fear and aggression. Conceiving in this way regularly, the mind began to foster those tendencies. In addition, physical repercussions from external sources were experienced, adding to the unpleasant feeling, and so on.

Speaking according to the conditions in this way, we have all the necessary information without the need for reference to Mr. Brown or any kind of self. The process contains in itself natural elements of various kinds arising and reacting with each other to produce actions and reactions, without the need for a doer or a receiver of results.

Whether speaking according to the conditions as given here, or according to the convention as related above, the reality of the situation is identical – neither is deficient or more complete – but the description of things as a natural condition is given in terms of the natural facts, without the appendages of conventional imagery.

In any case, even with these examples, there may still be some doubt on the matter, so it might be helpful to conclude with a story:

Tit Porng* went to visit the Venerable Abbot of the nearby monastery. At one point, he asked,

"Eh, Luang Por*, the Buddha taught that everything is not-self, and is without an owner – there is no-one who commits *kamma* and no-one who receives its results. If that's the case, then I can go out and hit somebody over the head or even kill them, or do anything I like, because there is no-one committing *kamma* and no-one receiving its results."

No sooner had Tit Porng finished speaking, when the Abbot's walking stick, concealed somewhere unknown to Tit Porng, swung

---

* Tit Porng: 'Tit' is a name given to one who has ordained as a bhikkhu for some time and later disrobed. 'Luang Por', literally meaning Reverend Father, is a term of respect given to venerated monks.

down like a flash. Tit Porng could hardly get his arm up fast enough to ward off the blow. Even so, the walking stick struck solidly in the middle of his arm, giving it a good bruise. Clutching his sore arm, Tit Porng said,

"Luang Por! Why did you do that?" His voice trembled with the anger that was welling up inside him.

"Oh! What's the matter?" the Abbot asked off-handedly.

"Why, you hit me! That hurts!"

The Abbot, assuming a tone of voice usually reserved for sermons, slowly murmured: "There is *kamma* but no-one creating it. There are results of *kamma*, but no-one receiving them. There is feeling, but no-one experiencing it. There is pain, but no-one in pain ... He who tries to use the law of not-self for his own selfish purposes is not freed of self; he who clings to not-self is one who clings to self. He does not really know not-self. He who clings to the idea that there is no-one who creates *kamma* must also cling to the idea that there is one who is in pain. He does not really know that there is no-one who creates *kamma* and no-one who experiences pain."

The moral of this story is: if you want to say 'there is no-one who creates *kamma*', you must first learn how to stop saying 'Ouch!'

7 IN CONCLUSION

T HE PRACTICAL objective of the teaching of *kamma* can be summarized thus:

1) To establish an understanding firmly based on reason, looking at actions and their results in terms of cause and effect, rather than clinging to lucky charms and auspicious objects.

2) This in turn will demonstrate the success of any aspiration as being dependent on action, encouraging self-reliance and diligence.

3) To develop a sense of responsibility – to one self by giving up bad actions, and towards others by acting kindly towards them.

4) To nurture the understanding that all individuals have a natural and equal right, either to let themselves degenerate, or to improve and develop themselves.

5) To understand that mental qualities, abilities and behaviour are the measuring sticks of human baseness or refinement. Discrimination according to caste or race are unnecessary and harmful.

6) To learn from old *kamma* (past actions), knowing how to consider and understand actions according to reason, not simply finding fault with others or external situations, but looking into one's own actions in the present moment, ascertaining how to correct and improve oneself and determining the most useful actions for any given situation.

7) Putting the future, in the form of personal responsibility, back into the hands of each individual.

These values can be considered in the light of the Buddha's

words presented here:

The general meaning

"*Bhikkhus*, intention, I say, is *kamma*. With intention as the forerunner, *kamma* is created through body, speech and mind."[48]

"All beings are the owners of their *kamma*, heirs to their *kamma*, born of their *kamma*, related to their *kamma*, supported by their *kamma*. *Kamma* it is which separates beings into coarse and refined states."[49]

"Whatever seed one plants, one reaps the fruit thereof. Who does good receives good, who does evil receives evil."[50]

"The fool treats himself like an enemy, creating bad *kamma*, a cause for misery. On account of whatever *kamma* one experiences distress, a face wet with tears and distraction, that is not good *kamma*."[51]

"On account of whatever *kamma* one experiences no distress, but a heart bright and cheerful, that is good *kamma*. Knowing what *kamma* is useful, one should quickly act thereon."[51]

Intelligence over superstition

"If it were possible to cleanse evil *kamma* simply by bathing in a river, then the frogs, fish, otters, crocodiles and other river-dwelling animals would certainly be destined for rebirth in a heaven realm ... If these rivers were capable of carrying your evil *kamma* away, then they could probably also carry away your good *kamma*."[52]

"Benefit slips by while the fool counts the stars. Benefit is the harbinger of benefit, of what use are the stars?"[53]

"For whosoever there is right action, that is a favourable time, an auspicious time, an auspicious morning, an auspicious dawning, an auspicious moment, an auspicious occasion; and in that action there is veneration of the holy. The bodily *kamma*

... verbal *kamma* ... mental *kamma* of such a one are auspicious, and his wishes are auspicious. Having created auspicious *kamma*, that person experiences only auspicious results."[54]

Action rather than invocation

"Yearn neither for the past, nor anticipate the future. The past is gone, the future yet to come. He who sees clearly the present moment, certain and unwavering, should strive to maintain that awareness. Practise diligently today, who knows whether tomorrow will bring death? No-one can bargain with the Lord of Death and his hordes. One who practises in such a way, even for one night, ardent, lazy neither day nor night, is praised by the Peaceful One*."[55]

"Listen, householder, these five conditions are desirable, worthy of favour, worthy of pleasure, and are hard to come by in this world. They are longevity ... pleasant appearance ... happiness ... status ... heaven. These five conditions, I say, are not to be had by mere supplication or aspiration. If these five conditions were obtainable through mere supplication or aspiration, then who in this world would not have them? Listen, householder, the Noble Disciple, desiring long life, should not waste his time supplicating or merely delighting in the wish for longevity. The Noble Disciple desiring longevity should maintain the practice which produces longevity. Only the practice which produces longevity is capable of procuring longevity. That Noble Disciple will thus be one who has longevity, both divine and human ... he who desires pleasant appearance ... happiness ... status ... heaven, should develop the practice which produces pleasant appearance ... happiness ...status ... heaven ..."[56]

"*Bhikkhus*, even though a *bhikkhu* were to conceive the wish, 'May my mind be freed from the *Āsava*,' if he does not diligently devote himself to the training of the mind, he will be

---

* Muni – An epithet of the Buddha.

unable to free the mind from the *Āsava*. Just like a mother hen who refuses to sit on her eggs, to warm, to incubate them. Even though that hen might conceive the wish, 'May my babies, using their feet and beaks, break out safely from these eggs,' it would be impossible for those chicks to do so."[57]

Non-adherance to race or class

"I do not say that one becomes a Brahmin on emerging from the mother's womb. That is simply what the Brahmins say. Such a person still has defilements. I say that it is rather the one who has no defilements and without clinging who is Brahmin.

"Name and family established in this world are merely worldly conventions. They arise from the speech based on views adhered to over the ages by ignorant beings. Those ignorant beings say they are Brahmins because of their birth. But one does not become either Brahmin or non-Brahmin through birth. One is a Brahmin through action* (*kamma*), is a non-Brahmin through action. One is a farmer through action, one is an artist through action, a merchant through action, a servant through action, a thief through action, a King through action. The wise, skilled in the *Paṭiccasamuppāda*, understanding *kamma* and its results, understand *kamma* clearly as it is ... that the world proceeds according to *kamma*, all beings fare according to *kamma*. Beings are bound together by *kamma*, just as a running cart is bound by its couplings."[58]

"One is not evil because of birth, and is not a Brahmin because of birth, but is evil because of *kamma*, and is a Brahmin because of *kamma*."[59]

"Any person from among these four castes, the Warrior, the Brahmin, thè merchants and the menials, having left home and gone forth in the Teaching and Discipline of the *Tathāgata*, dispenses with name and family, and all become equally recluses,

---

* This is *kamma* in its sense of 'work' or 'profession'.

Sons of the Sakyans."[60]

"From among these four castes, any who have become *bhikkhus*, freed of the *Āsava*, who have completed the training, done what was to be done and laid down the burden; who have attained the true benefit, the freedom from the fetters, liberation through true wisdom ... they are more excellent than any of those castes."[61]

Self reliance

"You must do the practice yourselves. The *Tathāgata* only points the way."[62]

"Self is the mainstay of self, who else could be your mainstay? Having trained the self well, one attains a mainstay hard to come by."[63]

"Purity and impurity are personal responsibilities. No one else can make you pure."[64]

"*Bhikkhus*, be a refuge unto yourselves, do not cling to anything else. Take the Dhamma as your refuge, take nothing else as your refuge."[65]

A caution for the future

"Women, men, laypeople and homeless ones* should regularly reflect that, 'We are the owners of our *kamma*, the heirs of our *kamma*, born of our *kamma*, descended from our *kamma*, supported by our *kamma*. Whatever *kamma* is done by us, whether good or bad, we will receive the results thereof.'"[66]

"If you fear suffering, do not make bad *kamma*, either in public or in private. If you make bad *kamma*, even if you fly into the air, you will be unable to escape suffering."[67]

"Grain, possessions, money, all your cherished things, servants, employees and associates ... none of these can you take with you, you must cast them all aside.

---

* Homeless Ones – i.e., those ordained into the Buddhist monastic order.

"But whatever *kamma* is made by you, whether by body, speech or mind, that is your real possession, and you must fare according to that *kamma*. That *kamma* will follow you, just as the shadow follows its owner."

"Therefore, do good actions, gather benefit for the future. Goodness is the mainstay of beings in the hereafter."[68]

REFERENCES

The references given first are from the Pali Text Society's version of the *Pali Tipitaka,* while those in brackets are from the Thai *Siam-raṭṭha* version of the same.

1   Sn. 654 (M.13/707/648; Sn.25/382/457)
2   A.III.415 (A.22/334/464)
3   J.IV.390 (J.27/2054/413)
4   It.25 (It.25/208-9/248-9)
5   Sn.612-654 (M.13/707/643-9; Sn.25/382/451-8)
6   M.I.373 (M.13/64/56)
7   M.III.72 (M.14/258/181)
8   A.I.30 (A.20/182/40)
9   A.I.32 (A.20/189-190/42-43)
10 A.I.33 (A.20/191-3/44)
11 Dh.1-3 (Dh.25/11/15)
12 Dhs.181 (Dhs.34/663/259)
13 Nd¹12, 360, 467; Nd²199 (Nd¹29/22/14-18; 728/436-441; 911/573-8; Nd²30/692/348-352)
14 S.I.70, 98; It.45 (S.15/329/101; 404/143; It.25/228/264)
15 S.I.98 (S.15/403/142)
16 A.I.201 (A.20/509/258-263)
17 A.I.263 (A.20/551/338)
18 A.I.189 (A.20/505/243)
19 M.II.114 (M.13/553-4/500-3)
20 A.I.216 (A.20/511/278-9)
21 Dh.71 (Dh.25/15/24)
22 Dh.172 (Dh.25/23/38)
23 S.I.37 (S.15/163/51)
24 A.I.57 (A.20/264/73)
25 A.I.58 (A.20/265/74)

26 A.V.39 (A.24/23/41)

27 S.I.227; J.II.199, III.157 (S.15/903/333; J.27/294/84; 713/166)

28 Vbh.338 (Vbh.35/840/458-9)

29 M.III.203 (M.14/579-597/376-385)

30 D.I.92 (D.11/62-63/101-2)

31 D.I.70 (D.11/45/77)

32 D.I.230; M.I.389; A.II.230-237 (D.11/256/242; M.13/88/82; A.21/232-8/ 313-322)

33 M.II.214; M.193; A.I.220 (M.14/3/2; M.12/219/185; A.20/514/284)

34 A.III.415 (A.22/334/464)

35 S.III.132 (S.18/227-230/166)

36 S.II.64 (S.16/143/77)

37 A.I.134 (A.20/473/171)

38 A.I.263; *cf.* A.I.264; A.III.338 (A.20/551/338; *cf.*A.20/552/339; A.22/310/ 378)

39 A.V.261 (A.24/163/282)

40 A.II.233 (A.21/235/318)

41 S.V.86 (S.19/450/123)

42 A.I.173; *cf.*Vbh.367; M.II.214 (A.20/501/222; *cf.*Vbh.35/940/496; M.14/ 2-11/1-13)

43 M.II.214 (M.14/2/1)

44 S.IV.230 (S.18/427/284)

45 A.I.249 (A.20/540/320)

46 S.IV.319 (S.18/613-9/393-398)

47 M.III.19; S.III.104 (M.14/129/106; S.17/192/126)

48 A.III.415 (A.22/334/464)

49 M.III.203 (M.14/579/376)

50 S.I.227 (S.15/903/333)

51 S.I.57 (S.15/281/81)

52 Thīg.240-244 (Thīg.26/466/473)

53 J.I.257 (J.27/49/16)

54 A.I.294 (A.20/595/379)

55 M.III.187 (M.14/527/348)

56 A.III.47 (A.22/43/51)

57 S.III.153 (S.17/261/186)

58 Sn.620, 648-654 (M.13/707/645; Sn.25/382/453)
59 Sn.142 (Sn.25/306/352)
60 A.IV.203 (A.23/109/205)
61 D.III.97 (D.11/71/107)
62 Dh.276 (Dh.25/30/51)
63 Dh.160 (Dh.25/22/36)
64 Dh.165 (Dh.25/22/37)
65 D.II.100; D.III.77; S.III.42 (D.10/94/119; D.11/49/84; S.17/87/53)
66 A.III.71 (A.22/57/82)
67 Ud.51 (Ud.25/115/150)
68 S.I.93 (S.15/392/134)

A.	=	Anguttara-nikāya
D.	=	Dīgha-nikāya
Dh.	=	Dhammapada
Dhs.	=	Dhammasangani
It.	=	Itivuttaka
J	=	Jātaka
M.	=	Majjhima-nikāya
Nd¹	=	(Mahā-)Niddesa
Nd²	=	(Cūla-) Niddesa
S.	=	Samyutta-nikāya
Sn.	=	Suttanipāta
Ud.	=	Udāna
Vbh.	=	Vibhanga

INDEX

J

Jain. *See* Niganthas
jhāna   20

K

Whatever actions we do,
Whether good or evil,
Of that kamma we will be the heirs

NAMES OF SPONSORS.

K. L.

$100

CHEONG WOON KWAI
LEE ENG HOCK (IM)
REV C K

$50

LAU BENG LONG
NEW AI HONG & FLY
NG YAN TIN
SEE AH SIEW
TEOH KIAN KOON & FLY
WOOI KHENG CHOO
YOW CHEW LIN

$30

ANONYMOUS
CHEONG YEE SOON
FOONG ERIC
TAN CHIN THENG
WEE FAMILY

$23

KUAN TUCK WAN

$20

CHAN SIEW YEAN (IM)
GOH K H
KUA KEAN SOON
LAU PING CHENG
LIM BOON CHUNG
NG AGNES
OO KHAIK CHEANG
THAM SEE LIN & FLY
Y C K
YONG YEW CHOON (IM)

$15

ANONYMOUS DR
LAU SEE TIAK
TAN FAMILY

$13

LEE RICHARD & FLY
LOH KEA YU & FLY

$10

ANONYMOUS
AW KIM FATT
AW SING CHUNG
BAMPHEN
CHAN AH WAI
CHAN CHRISTINE
CHAN MICHAEL
CHAN VICTOR
CHAN S A
CHAN WAH SING
CHANG NYUK GIN
CHAW NGAI HOONG
CHEAH BOON KUAN & FLY
CHEONG CHEE BUN & FLY
CHEONG KUM THONG
CHEONG KUM YIN
CHEONG YEE YOKE
CHEW LILY & FLY
DAVID M
FOO AH SEE & FLY
FUN YEW KHEONG
HO PENG CHUEN & FLY
KHOO CHOO KEAT
KIEU CHOO LAI
KUAN NYUK LING
KUAN TUCK KHEONG
LAI TUCK CHEE & FLY
LAU FONG KUNG
LEE LIP MENG
LENG PAK CHEW
LIM CHEE BENG & FLY
LIM IVY
LIM POH ENG
LIM SHIREEN
LING AI ING & FLY
MANIKAM T K
MEE SONG PHRA
NG CATHERINE
NG HIANG PENG
NG FOO MUN
ONG HOCK EANG & FLY
ONG MEE LEONG
ONG NGAI & FLY
OOI PAU LEE
PAPUMA UTTARAYA
SELVARAJU DATO DR
SIM MONG HENG
T T & FAMILY
TAN BOON KEONG & FLY
TAN C H
TAN EYE TEONG & FLY

$10 (Cont')

TAN KWYE HOE (IM)
TAN SENG LOON & FLY
TEH CANON
TEH RICHARD
TEH HEONG PENG
TEOH JAYA
TEY CHIN LAM
WEE KIAT
WONG JEANNE
YAP FOOI FOONG
YEONG CHET YEI
YEOW PHILIP

$5

CHAN ELLEN
CHEAH KHEEMA
FOO CHOOI KEE
KHOO CHOO BENG
LAU YON LAI
LEN PAT MOOI
PANG KONG HWA
PUN YEW CHEONG
TEH BENG HOCK
TEH CAROLINE
TEH MICHELLE
THEAN KHOOK YIN
TSAO KHEE MIAG
YAP FELICIA
YEO BOBBY

$3

CHEONG KUM THO
CHEONG KUM WAH
CHEONG SIEW KOW
CHEONG SIEW SENG
CHONG YEAN FOON
CHUAH MOOI HOON
KOK ADELAINE
KOK LAURENCE
KRIS
LOH HIN LEONG
LOH YOKE KHOON
PUN CHEE LEONG
PUN SUK MUN
PUN YOKE LEONG
YEAH LIAN WAH

WOCBK

$200

PENANG TRIP GROUP

$50

LEE FOOK SUNG & FLY
OOI CHOK SENG
TUES CHANTING CLASS
YONG KAN CHOO & FLY

$30

KOK HOONG & FLY

$20

LIM MEE SEW
LOW LEE LIM
OOI SOON KOK & FLY
SU SUI KOON
SU YIN MDM (IM)
YONG THIAM FAM

$10

CHENG LEE YING
CHAIN DOLLY
KHOR THANG KIEW & FLY
LAU SIAU LING
LAU TWEI YEAN
LEONG BEE KIEW
LIM TIANG CHU & FLY
NG GEAK ENG
PANG SWEE KEW
SAU AH MOOI
TAN BONG CHING
TAN LO SEONG
TAN NGUK LUAN
TEH KIM KEE &
PUAH MUAH (IM)
TOH ROBERT
WONG KIAN MENG

$5

CHAN HON KEONG
CHENG LIEW LIM (IM)
CHEONG YEE YOKE
CHONG YOON SIONG
FONG LISA
LEE M

$5 (Cont'd)

LIM ENG SIM (IM)
ONG BENG HOE (IM)
ONG P Y
WONG SWEE FOONG

WYY

$10

CHOW YOON KHEN
HUE SIEW KIOW & FLY
TOCK TUTU
WEE KEE HONG
WOO CHAI LENG & FLY

$5

CHEW BEE LAU
CHOONG RITA
CHUA C K
HAM PENG HENG
HOW KIM LEONG
HOR MEI FONG
LAW TAN NEE
LEE HO & FLY
LIM GUAT MEY & FLY
NG ENG SIEW
OOI BENG HWA & FLY
PHOON FOOK
SIEW RICHARD
TAN YONG HIN
TAY SIEW WAH
TIEW GEK ENG
YEOH LEANNE

$2

CHUA T S
KHONG M S
LEE BAN SING
LEE SUSAN
OOI GEOK GOK
WOO LIAN KONG
WOO TONY
WOO YEN YEN
YU M S

LC

$30

紀念莊啓兆
紀念林素好
紀念莊壬水
紀念陳彩屏
紀念莊粉音

$20

CHING KIM SIAH
CHING LOY HANN
CHING LOY HUAH
CHING LOY NGUAN
CHING LOY YANG
CHING MANG KHENG
CHING SEE TEE
CHING SOOK FONG
CHING SOOK GINN
CHING YEW MING
CHONG KWI YIN
LING LEONG KIEW
LOW FONG PANG

KLANG

$10

KIANG HSIANG SHENG

K. TRENGGANU

$200

ANONYMOUS

$20

FONG SEE YEW (IM)

$10

CHOO GEOK LIAM (IM)
DAM DWA NGOH
FONG JONG HWA
FONG J K
PANG BOH WAH

MALACCA

$100

QUEK POH CHUAN & FLY
TOH SISTER

$50

CHEE JERRY & FLY
LEONG HO SUM & FLY
TAN CHEE NYA (IM)
TAN KIAN SIONG (IM)

$25

ANG FAMILY
LWEE WAN TIONG

$20

ANONYMOUS
CHAN LEONG HUAT
CHEE MOLLY
LIM P G
OH KIM LENG & FLY
SEOW WEI LUN
SOH MENG HUANG
TAI
TAI EK CHIAN
TAN BOH JONG
TANG L C & FLY
TEOH KIM LIAN & FLY
TEOH KIM SIONG

$10

AU SU JOO CHOO
CHAN DORIS
FOO ERIC & FLY
HO CHEW CHYE & FLY
KHO CHEN CHEE
KOH GEOK ENG
LEE FATT CHUAN & FLY
LEE KHON IT & FLY
LEE YOON FOO (IM)
LEO KIM LIAM
LEO KIM MOI
LIM C T
LIM SOO CHOW & FLY
LYE KIM YONG & FLY
NGIM CHEN PENG
ONG B S
ONG LOW SIANG

$10 (Cont)

ONN RUBY
TAM BEE YOKE
TAN CHO TIM
TEH GEK SENG & FLY
THUM SUM CHOY
WEE FAMILY
WOON CHER YOON
YEO TAI WAH

$5

ANONYMOUS
CHAN PENG YEEN
CHAI GEK MIN
HO MOLLY
LIM KIEN KOK
ONG VICTOR
SEOW GRACE
TAN P H
THAM CHEE HOI
WONG STEPHENINE
YOONG CHAI YOONG

PERAK

$100

LIM PENG SWEE

$50

SUM YEE (IM)

$10

CHAN TAT SENG
CHONG PIK NYUK
EWE POH NYA MDM
EWE SIEW CHOON
EWE SIEW YONG

TELUK INTAN

$50

KAM YONG (IM)

$30

TEH LAI ENG

$20

YAP FAMILY

$10

CHONG CHEE KEONG & FLY
CHONG K L & FLY
LEE CHOO SIK
LIM SAW GHIM
OH TEIK BIN
OOI HEAN BENG
TAN LAI LOON
TOH CINDY
WONG SOK CHAN

$5

LOH AH LOOY
OH JOHNNY

PENANG

$100

T C LIM & FLY

$20

LIM SIANG HOR & FLY
QUAH KUNG SUN & FLY

$10

ANONYMOUS
KHOO BENG KEE & FLY
TANG SEOK HOO & FLY
TEOH BOON TAT

$5

SOO MING SHEN
SOO LI YING
SOO POOI SUM
TAN SUAN HEOW

BUKIT MERTAJAM

$50

CHEAH SOO JIN & FLY
KHAW LEK AI
KHAW LOKE TEE

KEDAH

$50

WONG SEE CHIANG
WONG WAI LOONG
WONG YEE LIN

KUCHING

$100

TEH CHEOK KOOI (IM)
TEO AH HIOK

$50

BONG SHIAW WEE JENNIFER
JONG LEE FAH
JONG LEE PHIN & FLY
JONG SAY MOI & FLY
JONG KHENG CHUAN MR/S

$40

GOH GEOK BOI

$20

JONG KAH YIN & FLY
JONG LEE CHIN & FLY
JONG LI PING
TEOH ENG HO & FLY

$10

BONG NYUK HIONG
GOH ENG TONG (IM)
JONG LEE KIAN & FLY
TAN KORNIE
TAN RICKY & FLY
TAN YAM THONG (IM)
THO KAY HUA

$9

CHUA KARUNA

$8

BONG SHAO FANG

$5

GOH CHUI SENG FRANCIS
GOH SIAW NOI
JONG DORIS & FLY
JONG GEE ANN
LING JIN HIOK
TAN AINEE
TAN JIANN YIK ERIC
TAN WAN HUA
TAN WANN YIE GFRALDINE
THONG AI HUA

$3

GOH KIM LAN
SU THOMAS & FLY
THONG JULIA

$2

CHONG GEORGE
CHONG PAUL
CHONG VICTOR
FANG CHIK CHIN
GOH CHIEW TOH
GOH CHUI KING
GOH HANG BOON
GOH MOH HENG
GOH YIAN NEE
GOH YIAN YIAN
GUAN GUAK HUA
JEE CHIEW NGO
LING HIOK KHENG
LINH KHIA HIOK
SIA CHIN SIANG
TAY MEI YAW

SABAH

$100

CHIU SHENG BIN

$50

FOO SUE

LABUAN

$50

PHOON SAU HENG

SINGAPORE

$100

LEE LIAN HOON (IM)